THE UNNECESSARY EVIL

THE UNNEC

RUBEN BELLAN

=SSARY EVIL

An Answer to Canada's High Unemployment

McClelland and Stewart

McClelland and Stewart Limited
The Canadian Publishers
481 University Avenue
Toronto, Ontario
M5G 2E9

Canadian Cataloguing in Publication Data

Bellan, R.C. (Ruben Carl), 1918–
    The unnecessary evil

ISBN 0-7710-1153-9

1. Unemployment – Canada.   2. Unemployment – History
– Canada.   I.   Title.

HD5728.B44 1986   331.13'7971   C86-094244-9

Printed and bound in Canada by John Deyell Printing Co.

Contents

To Ruth

Acknowledgments

Acknowledgments on my part are very much in order. To colleagues in economics, and in other disciplines as well, I owe thanks for suggestions and observations. I am especially indebted to Professors Norman Cameron and Lovell Clark for their reading of an earlier draft. Joyce Laird typed the several drafts and numerous revisions with her customary skill and dedication.

Introduction

For the entire decade of the 1930s the Canadian economy wallowed in the worst depression in history. The unemployment rate averaged about 15 per cent; in 1932 it was a catastrophic 22 per cent. World War II, which began in 1939, brought a dramatic transformation. By 1941, once the war effort had reached high gear, severe unemployment was replaced by a critical labour shortage. The armed forces enlisted every able-bodied male who volunteered for military service and would have gladly taken in more; the thousands of firms that had war orders eagerly sought workers; firms producing civilian goods and services, experiencing strong demand because of the general prosperity, hired practically whomever they could get.

This galvanization of the Canadian economy from sluggishness to hyperactivity was achieved by the federal government's enormous spending. It was the government that provided the pay of the hundreds of thousands of persons who served in the armed forces and merchant marine; it was the government that paid the contractors who built the hundreds of air fields, training camps, and barrack blocks; it was the government that bought the immense amount of war material produced by Canadian industry.

The government could have spent money on this scale previously; war did not provide it with financial capability that it had not possessed in peacetime. It had refrained, however, forbidden by an economic orthodoxy that warned both that it was impossible and that the results would be catastrophic. First, declared the experts, Canada simply didn't have the money; it would have to be obtained from foreign sources – and they would no doubt refuse to supply it. Secondly, a large addition to the country's monetary circulation would inevitably cause a ruinous inflation. Finally, the burden of debt assumed by the government in borrowing the money would oppress the country ever after.

Canada could expect a restoration of prosperity, the experts proclaimed throughout the 1930s, only when private enterprise saw fit to invest on a large scale in new industrial plant whose future product would repay the investment. It would be ruinous folly for the government to attempt to make up the current and prospective deficiency of jobs in the country by additional spending on public works and public services.

Wartime experience shatteringly refuted every one of the orthodoxies that had forbidden a determined government program to liquidate the calamitous unemployment of the 1930s. The vast sums spent by the government on the war effort were raised entirely within Canada, provided by Canadian taxpayers and savers and the Canadian banking system; not one cent was needed from outside the country. The expenditures were for purposes that had absolutely no economic value and were in fact worse than merely wasteful, because they were intentionally destructive. The enormous increase in monetary circulation during the war did not result in wild inflation: the price level rose by less than 2 per cent a year, and that increase was attributable, quite clearly, to shortages of civilian goods inevitable in wartime. The country was not crushed afterwards by the government's debt burden; the people of Canada were in fact far better off in the post-war era, when the national debt was immensely larger, than they had been in the 1930s, when it had been only about $4 billion.

The doctrines of half a century ago, categorically disproven by actual experience, have once again become part of the conventional wisdom. While over 1.5 million Canadians are without work and likely to remain so for years, we are warned that any attempt by government to create employment for them would be dangerous folly. The new federal government elected in 1984, instead of increasing spending to generate jobs, has reduced spending in order to hold down the debt owed by the people of Canada to themselves, a debt declared to be an intolerably oppressive burden on the country. The inflation that has been experienced in recent years is attributed to excessive increase in spending, when it's glaringly obvious that costs, and therefore prices, were in fact pushed up by Arab oil-sellers, by corporations with great market power, and by workers who were better educated, had higher self-esteem, and were better organized than workers in the past. Against inflation that stemmed from such causes, the fiscal and monetary restraints dictated by economic orthodoxy have been grotesquely inappropriate. They severely aggravated the problem of unemployment and, ironically, probably aggravated the inflation problem as well.

As wartime experience convincingly demonstrated, it's perfectly possible for Canada to have full employment without inflation. What is needed is government action to assure that the aggregate of spending in the country is sufficient, together with arrangements to prevent wages and profits from rising by more than national productivity. Admittedly, we cannot expect that the wage, profit, and price controls that served well in wartime would be tolerated in peacetime. The critical need is for arrangements that would be acceptable in peacetime and would have the same stabilizing effect on the price level as controls had in wartime. A number of procedures have already been attempted; several others are suggested here; more no doubt can be conceived. It should not be beyond our ingenuity to devise means of preventing inflationary wage and profit increases that are preferable to the brutal club of unemployment. It should not be beyond our capacity for compromise and accord to apply them.

This book is a plea for a more humane – and less wasteful – economic policy. It is written by someone who has a greater respect for the free enterprise system than do champions of free enterprise who insist that it is incapable of providing useful employment for all Canadians who seek it.

ONE

Unemployment—and Inflation

Lost time is never found again.
AUGHEY

Since 1982 the number of unemployed persons in Canada has at all times been in excess of a million; at all times about one worker in ten has been jobless. This is a much higher level of unemployment than that which Canada experienced for a good many years.

In the three decades from 1946 to 1975 the unemployment rate averaged just over 4 per cent; in only one year was it above 7 per cent. The rise in the unemployment rate to its present level occurred in two quite distinct stages: it rose from 5.4 per cent in 1974 to 7.1

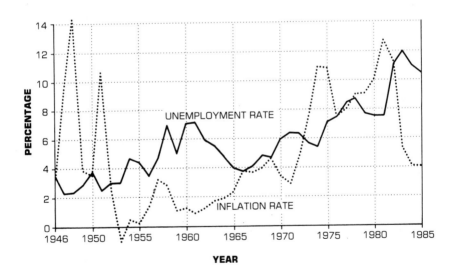

Canada's Inflation and Unemployment, 1946—85

SOURCE: Statistics Canada

per cent in 1975, and again from 7.5 per cent in 1981 to 11.0 per cent in 1982. Since then it has remained in the 10- to 11-per-cent range.

The official definition of an unemployed person is someone who has looked for a job in the four weeks before a given survey but was unable to get one. The official figures, therefore, do not include those who would have liked to work but didn't look for a job in the previous four weeks because they felt it would have been a waste of time. If these people are counted in, then the number of Canadians who have wanted to work but couldn't get jobs has constantly been, since 1982, in the neighbourhood of 1.5 million.

These people are capable of doing useful work and want to be employed instead of idle. Why are there no jobs for them?

The reason is simple. Anyone who has a job works either for a private employer or for some public body. Businesses hire people only when they expect to sell at a profit what employees will produce. Public authorities hire people to provide services only when they believe the public wants those services and is prepared to pay for them through taxation. If some workers can't get jobs it's because private employers don't think they could profitably sell what those workers would produce for them, and public authorities don't think that voters are willing to pay the higher taxes that would have to be levied if more people were hired to build public works or to provide public services.

The production of the private sector falls into three broad categories: consumption goods – the food, clothing, shelter, entertainment, and so on that the general public buys; investment goods – the buildings, machinery, and equipment that businesses buy for the purpose of production; and goods for export – the wheat, newsprint, lumber, minerals, and other products that foreigners buy from us.

The spending on every one of these categories varies from year to year. The general public sometimes increases its spending on consumption goods because people have higher incomes, because they feel more confident, because they are attracted by new products, and so on. Businesses build new plant and acquire more equipment because they expect to have larger sales in the future, because they want to produce new products that promise good profits, because rich deposits of valuable natural resources have been discovered, because a reduction in interest rates has made it cheaper to borrow money. Foreigners may buy more from Canada because they have had poor crops and need more food, because they have more money with which to buy, because they are expanding their industrial production and need more of our raw materials, because other countries that also produce our types of exports have less to sell.

In one year these influences may be generally upbeat, so that the aggregate of private-sector spending is large. Businesses will then need a great many workers to produce all the goods for which there is a profitable demand. In another year the influences on spending may be downbeat, so that the total of private-sector spending is small; businesses, their sales low, will need few employees.

Governments – federal, provincial, and municipal – also vary the amount of their spending. When population growth occurs, they must provide services to more people. The people may demand additional public services and improvement in the quality of those already being provided. Government spending is heavy while major works are being constructed, works such as power plants, roads, and water supply systems; spending declines when they are completed. Spending by the national government on the armed forces rises sharply during periods of international tension and soars to astronomic levels in wartime.

There is never a guarantee that the total number of persons whom private and public employers wish to employ will equal the number of persons seeking jobs. During both world wars more workers were wanted than were available. In peacetime it has usually been the other way around, with the number of jobs considerably lower than the number of persons seeking work. The shortfall of jobs was relatively small in the 1950s and 1960s but became noticeably larger in the 1970s and very large in the 1980s.

At any given time employers offer some jobs that go unfilled because unemployed persons don't have the skills required or aren't prepared to move to where the jobs are. The evidence indicates, however, that this "structural unemployment," as it is called by economists, has been a relatively small portion of the total. By far the most important reason why about 1.5 million Canadians have not been able to get work in the last few years is that there have not been enough jobs in Canada.

The degree of job shortage has typically varied with the season of the year. Some of Canada's leading industries – agriculture, fishing, construction, tourism – are slack during the winter and employers in these industries don't need workers, and no one else does either.

The job shortage has not been evenly distributed across the country; the unemployment rate has typically been higher in the Atlantic provinces and Quebec than elsewhere in Canada. People who were born and brought up in the East have preferred to stay in a familiar, congenial environment, even if it provides less work opportunity. In the case of Quebeckers, the desire to stay in familiar surroundings is reinforced by the fact that if they moved away they would be amid people of a different culture, who speak a different language.

Other regions of the country have on occasion experienced severe job shortages. The unemployment rate soared in Alberta in 1982 following a sharp decline in world oil prices and the introduction of new federal policies that burdened the oil industry. The number of unemployed persons swelled in British Columbia in 1983 when the market for lumber declined and the provincial government applied tight restraints on its spending.

Several distinct categories of persons bear the brunt of the persistent job shortage in Canada. Employers, hiring only about ninety of every hundred available workers, naturally choose the ninety who they believe will make the best employees. They therefore tend not to hire older persons, people over fifty. Workers of that age are likely to have less physical strength than younger persons, might be more difficult to train, will not stay as long with the firm, and will draw on its pension plan sooner.

Employers tend not to hire very young persons either, teenagers and persons in their early twenties: they are immature and lack experience. What's more, even if a younger person could do a job as well as, or better than, a somewhat older person, that older person might have "seniority": the job would belong to him as long as he handles it acceptably, even if someone comes along who can do it better.

A high rate of unemployment in Canada has become accepted, in a few short years, as a settled feature of the Canadian economy. There is general agreement among experts that the 10- to 12-per-cent unemployment rate that materialized in 1982 will continue indefinitely. Almost no one expects the rate to decline to the 3- to 5-per-cent range of the 1950s and 1960s. During the depression of the 1930s, the number of persons without work and seeking jobs averaged about 15 per cent of the country's total labour force; what is now being widely predicted, in effect, is that unemployment in

Canada will be at a level not far below that of the dismal 1930s for years to come.

There is a fundamental difference, however, between the nature of today's unemployment and that of the 1930s. Then the majority of the unemployed were heads of families; when they had no jobs, they were unable to support the families that were dependent on them. In addition, most of the persons who could not earn money had to seek public assistance. Today, on the other hand, the majority of the unemployed are young people living on their own and wives, sons, and daughters living at home, earning a second or third family income. Loss of a job does not entail privation for them. What's more, a person who becomes unemployed today gets financial support without stigma, in the form of unemployment insurance. Unemployment today does not inevitably demean people as it did in the 1930s, when almost all unemployed married men had to seek public welfare for themselves and their families, and unemployed single men were fed in soup kitchens and put up in camps.

It's true that some unemployed people who use up their unemployment insurance benefits have to ask for public assistance, and there are individuals and families today who depend on free food and free meals given out by charitable organizations. Their exact number is not known, but it is fairly certain that they constitute only a small proportion of the unemployed.

Nevertheless unemployment is still a severe social problem. It represents waste and loss – loss of the output that could have been produced had people been working instead of idle. That loss is irretrievable. A lost day's labour can never be recovered: we will never have what could have been produced in that idle time. And while unemployment does not cause the same scale of psychic harm that it used to, it is still damaging. Many of the people who can't get work become despondent, frustrated, and bitter. Some give vent to their feelings by committing crimes; some become ill. Marriages break down and people take their own lives. In our affluent society the emotional hurt and the social problems caused by unemployment are probably its worst consequence, more damaging than the economic loss it causes in the form of goods that could have been produced but weren't.

A new problem – continuous inflation – emerged after World War II and became a matter of very serious concern. During the 1930s Canada, like all other industrialized countries, had experienced the opposite problem, deflation: the consumer price index had fallen by 29 per cent between 1929 and 1933, and while it rose after that year, it had not recovered its 1929 level when World War II broke out. There was much talk of "reflation" in the 1930s, somehow raising prices to their former level in order to restore profitability and thereby achieve an increase in production and employment.

Strong inflationary pressures developed during the war, arising from the combination of shortages of civilian goods and a great increase in the public's buying power. The government very quickly imposed price controls, however, and they were quite effective. The consumer price index rose by less than 8 per cent between 1941 and 1945, an average of less than 2 per cent a year. Some goods were sold at black market prices – where buyer and seller were both willing to risk breaking the law and the buyer was prepared to pay handsomely rather than do without. Naturally, there are no statistics on the scale of black market dealings, but all available evidence indicates that they were relatively small and had little effect on the overall price level.

The controls that had been imposed in wartime were lifted in 1947 and prices immediately shot up; the price level rose by 9.5 per cent that year and 14.3 per cent the next. By 1949, however, the situation had stabilized, and the consumer price index rose that year by only 3.8 per cent, even less the following year. The outbreak of the Korean War in 1950 brought a sharp escalation of prices, primarily because many canny shoppers, mindful of wartime shortages, hastened to lay in ample supplies of goods "before the hoarders got them all."

During the next fourteen years, however, through 1965, the average inflation rate was under 2 per cent; in one year, 1953, the price level actually fell. The inflation rate was significantly higher during the next seven years, averaging 4 per cent. But in the following ten-year period, from 1973 to 1982, the inflation rate surged to a new level that averaged 9.7 per cent; in five of those years it was over 10 per cent. It moderated to an average of about 5 per cent in the next three years.

This experience with inflation was deeply disturbing. Every decline in the dollar's buying power correspondingly reduced the purchasing power of persons with fixed incomes, such as pensioners, and reduced the real value of everybody's savings. The sharp escalation of the inflation rate after 1972 suggested the possibility of continuous inflation at the new rate and raised the distant spectre of a wild escalation of the kind that had occurred in Germany in 1923. The price level had risen in that country a trillion-fold, destroying the savings of millions of people and causing a virtual paralysis of the economy. It was this convulsive experience that had persuaded many Germans to support Adolf Hitler and his Nazi party.

The experience of inflation, and the prospect that it would continue and perhaps worsen, had seriously unsettling effects on economic activity. A prime concern of many people became to "hedge against inflation" – to translate their savings into forms whose market value would rise by at least the inflation rate, so that the real value of their savings would be preserved. Keen competition developed to buy whatever was regarded as a good "hedge against inflation," causing prices of these goods to soar.

Businesspeople became apprehensive about the future and held back on investment in new plants. More construction workers were therefore unemployed and the country did not acquire what would have been desirable enlargements of its productive capacity. Because of the harm it had already done and the harm it appeared likely to do in the future, a great many people believed inflation to be the country's foremost economic problem.

Unemployment and inflation have not been afflictions of nature like floods, droughts, tornadoes, and volcanic eruptions. They have been the consequences of human action. Had people acted differently there would have been much less – conceivably none or virtually none – of both unemployment and inflation.

Governments can affect the behaviour of the people subject to their jurisdiction. They can keep them from following intended courses of action; by persuasion, inducement, and compulsion they can get them to follow alternatives. A national government has nearly unlimited power over its subjects: it can require them to hand over in taxation whatever amounts it decides; it can compel them to give up their property for whatever compensation it chooses; it can absolutely prohibit any form of activity that it considers to be counter to the national interest. As well, it designates what is the country's lawful money and creates it in whatever quantity it considers appropriate.

A government that possesses such powers has the capability of altogether preventing both unemployment and inflation or, at least, of keeping them down to minimum levels. The government of Canada has in fact exercised that capability in wartime. It is the contention of this book that the government can prevent unemployment and inflation in peacetime as well, by procedures that would be fully consistent with the basic principles of our democratic, free enterprise society.

TWO

Conventional Diagnosis

*Economists are like theologians. . . . Every religion other than
their own is the invention of man, whereas their own is an
emanation from God.*
KARL MARX

The economic policies applied by governments have not been based
simply on the experiences and views of politicians. Political leaders
have generally consulted professional economists and have been in-
fluenced by the advice they have received. However, since economists
notoriously disagree with one another, the nature of the advice that
politicians receive depends on which economists they consult. The
economic policies applied by the Canadian government have, in general, reflected "establishment" views, probably held by the majority
of Canadian economists.

In 1945 the Canadian government undertook responsibility for assuring a high and stable level of employment in the country. The
undertaking, contained in a White Paper on employment and income,
was very similar to that of a White Paper issued by the British
government the previous year. These papers in effect announced the
adoption of the doctrines of the English economist John Maynard
Keynes, set forth in his path-breaking book *The General Theory of
Employment, Interest and Money*, published in 1936.

In that book Keynes had shown that the severe unemployment
then being experienced in Britain – and throughout the industrialized
world – was attributable to deficiency of spending. He had advocated,
accordingly, that the government adopt measures designed to increase the total of spending in the country and thereby generate the
additional jobs the country needed. His view was proved right by
wartime experience; quite clearly it was the massive spending by
governments during World War II that liquidated the unemployment
that had plagued the Western world throughout the 1930s.

The undertaking by a national government to assure full employment was a landmark in economic history. Before Keynes, it had been generally assumed that the government had little or no role to play in the operation of the economy. As a number of countries had already demonstrated, a government could bring on a ruinous inflation by wildly increasing the amount it printed of the national currency, but it could not, in the general view, prevent unemployment and depression. At most it might provide palliatives in the form of welfare assistance to the victims and perhaps a few small-scale public works projects that would provide temporary jobs for a small number of the unemployed.

The undertaking to assure full employment, as it turned out, did not commit a government to a single, specific, clearly defined course of action. For at any given time there were always a number of economic problems to be dealt with. In particular, inflation – the last thing anyone would have worried about in the 1930s – became a serious problem once World War II ended. The measures needed to assure full employment might aggravate the inflation problem. Different people would have different priorities. What's more, the ultimate consequences of any measure could never be known in advance. Finally, and perhaps most significant, different people had different views as to the causes of particular problems, so they advocated conflicting policies, all in the name of economic stabilization.

The perspectives developed by three men were widely accepted. There was general acknowledgment of the central point made by Keynes – that large-scale unemployment was attributable to insufficiency of spending. Views diverged widely, however, as to how the deficiency should be made up.

In his revolutionary book Keynes had addressed himself almost exclusively to the problem of depression, the central economic issue of the time. He died in 1946, before inflation came to be a matter of concern, and his references to it were few and casual. It was his followers who made the assumption that inflation was the exact opposite of depression and therefore was to be treated by measures that were the exact opposite of those called for by depression. In their view, if the remedy for depression was to increase the total of spending in the country, the remedy for inflation was to reduce it. If to counter depression, the government should increase its own spending and induce increase in private-sector spending by reducing its taxation, then to counter inflation, it should reduce its own spending and raise taxation in order to curtail private-sector spending. Enthusiastic adherents were confident that by appropriately timed and measured responses, by carefully calculated variations in its spending and taxation, the government could "fine-tune" the economy: it could keep it from deviating upward into inflation or downward into depression.

Professor Milton Friedman of the University of Chicago, having examined U.S. experience from 1867 to 1960, concluded that all rises and falls in the price level had been caused by changes in the country's money supply. He argued, therefore, that to stabilize the economy the authorities should do nothing more than regulate the size of the national money supply. If the growth rate of the money supply is always held to equality with the country's rate of productivity growth, he contended, then neither inflation nor unemployment can occur, certainly not on a significant scale or for an extended period of time. The government, in Friedman's view, should not adjust its spending in order to stabilize the economy; it should merely provide those public services that the country needs and that private enterprise cannot provide. Attempts to "fine-tune" the economy, by raising and lowering the level of government spending and taxation, would do more harm than good.

These views were widely hailed by monetary authorities and professional economists – Friedman was awarded the Nobel Prize for economics in 1976 – and have had considerable influence on policy. The monetary authorities of the U.S. and Canada have been firm adherents of Friedman's "monetarist" doctrines and have determinedly applied policies that incorporate his teachings.

While there are sharp differences between Keynesians and monetarists, they are in basic agreement on one fundamental issue: both sides take it for granted that inflation is caused by excessive spending. But they attribute that excess to different causes. Keynesians declare that if the total of spending in a country is excessive, the government must be spending too much, and the public, receiving large incomes out of which it saves very little, is also spending too much. Monetarists, on the other hand, insist that the total of spending in the country depends on the size of the money supply. If that total is excessive, it is because the money supply is too large.

In the jargon of the economist, both Keynesians and monetarists believe that inflation is always a "demand-pull" phenomenon – that is, that it is always the buyers of goods who are responsible for a rise in prices. The public, in their view, wants more goods than the amount available. Faced with the possibility that they will not get what they want – and liberally supplied with purchasing power – some people offer to pay more than the going price, rather than do without. As at auction sales, it is the competitive bidding of would-be buyers against one another that drives prices upward in the marketplace. The obvious remedy is to limit the total of spending in the country.

(A contrasting view, set forth in the next chapter, is that contemporary inflation is largely of the "cost-push" variety – that is, that prices rise because sellers of goods and services insist on being paid more than before. Some do this because their own costs have risen: materials cost more; employees, more knowledgeable and better organized, insist on higher wages. Businesses, possessed of great market power, raise their profit margins. For reasons such as these, buyers have to pay more than before; they are confronted with an inflation not of their own making.)

Professor A.W. Phillips of the London School of Economics, having examined British statistics for the period 1861 to 1957, noted that when the unemployment rate was low, the price level usually rose; and when the unemployment rate was high, the price level stayed the same or actually fell. This relationship did not exist in absolutely constant form every year; it was an average tendency only, and there were a good many years that did not conform. On the basis of his figures Phillips suggested that the British price level would likely remain stable only if the unemployment rate were just under 2.5 per cent. Any reduction in the unemployment rate below that figure would cause the price level to rise; the bigger the reduction in the rate of unemployment, the greater would be the rise in the price level. On the other hand, an unemployment rate of 5.5 per cent would bring a fall in the price level.

Subsequent writers elaborated on the relationship that Phillips first discerned. A "trade-off" was declared to exist between unemployment and inflation: the more there was of one, the less there was bound to be of the other. In every country, it was said, there existed a "natural rate of unemployment," and great difficulty would ensue if the actual unemployment rate ever fell below this "natural" level. A sophisticated version was the NAIRU – non-accelerating inflation rate of unemployment; if ever the actual unemployment rate of a country went below its NAIRU, the country's inflation rate would be bound to go up.

Each of the several diagnoses of the inflation problem implies its own brand of therapy. Keynesians and monetarists, while agreeing that inflation is caused by excessive spending, propose widely divergent remedial measures. Keynesians advocate "fiscal policy" measures – reductions in government spending together with increases in taxation to reduce the spending power of the public. Monetarists urge "monetary policy" measures – tight controls over the growth rate of the country's money supply to keep it closely in line with the output of goods and services. Those others who believe that inflation is being caused by excessive increases in wages and profits advocate "incomes policies" – measures to limit those increases to conform with growth in real output.

Monetarist thinking underlay a significant change in the law in 1966. Until that year federal legislation imposed a ceiling of 6 per cent on the "prime" interest rate, the rate charged by the chartered banks to their best customers. That ceiling sometimes caused an awkward problem when the Bank of Canada restricted the growth rate of the country's money supply. If the public wanted to borrow more than the chartered banks had available to lend, the banks would have to turn away people who wanted to borrow money, were good credit risks, and were willing to pay the market rate of interest. They would have to turn these people away simply because the tight money policy being applied by the Bank of Canada limited their lending power to a total that was less than the total that the people of Canada wanted to borrow. The people who were refused loans would be frustrated and angry; they would complain of discriminatory treatment by banks who were lending to others but not to them.

The issue had arisen on a number of occasions during the 1950s. The chartered banks, in several periods when the Bank of Canada was tightly limiting the money supply, were unable to provide borrowers with all the funds they wanted. Small businesses charged that the banks were lending only to the big firms that were their favoured customers. Prime Minister Diefenbaker threatened that if the banks continued to discriminate against small borrowers, his government would introduce legislation that would compel them to lend out their funds more fairly.

The problem would be eliminated if the interest rate were permitted to rise without any restraint. The reason is that most people, if they had to pay a higher interest rate, would want to borrow less; some would no longer want to borrow at all. A sufficient rise in the interest rate would cause such a reduction in the amount that the public wanted to borrow that the limited amount available would now be sufficient. Every firm that was prepared to pay the higher market rate of interest would be able to borrow all it wished. There would not be any frustrated would-be borrowers who were refused loans by the banks even though they offered good security and were willing to pay the market rate of interest.

In accordance with the recommendations of a royal commission, Parliament in 1966 removed the 6-per-cent ceiling on the prime interest rate. From then on, when the Bank of Canada applied tightly restrictive policies, the prime interest rate rose correspondingly.

Monetary restraints are applied by the country's central bank, the Bank of Canada, which is wholly owned by the federal government and whose governor and directors are appointed by the government. The Bank controls the size of the Canadian money supply. It creates our paper currency by printing a picture of the Queen or former prime ministers of Canada on slips of paper, adding an interesting Canadian scene on the other side. Those pieces of paper are the lawful money of Canada and must be accepted by any creditor in payment of a debt, because of the terse statement on them, above the signatures of the governor and deputy governor of the Bank of Canada, "This note is legal tender"; "Ce billet a cours légal."

The Bank also controls, through indirect means, the total of bank deposits. The chartered banks are required by law to keep cash reserves amounting to 10 per cent of their demand deposits – the deposits on which cheques can be written to make payments. These reserves must be in the lawful money of the country, which consists of deposits in the Bank of Canada and the paper currency it issues.

The Bank creates deposits in itself by buying federal government bonds, both directly from the government and from financial institutions that have previously acquired bonds and now wish to sell some. It pays for bond purchases by crediting the sellers with deposits in its books. Sellers of bonds transfer these deposits, by cheque, to whomever they choose. When a deposit in the Bank of Canada is credited to a chartered bank, that bank's legal cash reserves increase by that amount, and a multiple increase becomes possible in the deposits that Canada's banks have on their books. Thus if the Bank of Canada buys $1,000 of bonds, the $1,000 that it pays, in the form of a deposit in its books, increases the cash reserves of the chartered banks by $1,000 and their deposits may increase by $10,000.

On the other hand, if the Bank of Canada *sells* $1,000 of bonds, taking a cheque on a bank in payment, it deducts that amount from that bank's deposit on its books. The cash reserves of that bank are therefore reduced by $1,000, forcing a $10,000 reduction in the total of deposits in the chartered banks.

It is through its purchase and sale of federal government bonds that the Bank of Canada increases or decreases the Canadian money supply. With the virtually uninterrupted growth of the Canadian economy in the past half-century, and the nearly constant rise in prices, a larger money supply has been needed each year to make an ever-increasing volume of payments. Money has been "tight" in years when the Bank brought about an increase in the country's money supply that was smaller than the increase in demand; it has been plentiful when the Bank permitted an increase in the money supply that was as great as, or greater than, the increase in demand.

According to the Keynesian-monetarist views that have dominated economic thinking in Canada, the performance of the economy has depended primarily on the policies followed by the national authorities. If rates of inflation and unemployment were low in the 1950s and 1960s, it was because of the wise and temperate policies of the country's economic authorities. If rates of inflation and unemployment rose to alarming levels in the 1970s, it was primarily because of what those authorities did or failed to do. According to the widely accepted view, the government went on a wild spending spree, indicated by its huge budget deficits. As well, the public demanded far more than the economy was capable of producing; the government was blamed for failing to curb that demand by tax increases that would have held down the public's spending power. Monetary authorities were blamed for obligingly creating the additional money that fuelled the inflationary spending by both the government and the general public.

Gerald Bouey, governor of the Bank of Canada, expressed a generally held opinion in 1982 when, referring to what he called the "great inflation" of the 1970s, he declared: "Fundamentally it was caused by over-ambitious economic policies in general, and financial policies in particular. Nearly all countries drove their economic systems too hard, harder than they were capable of performing without generating inflationary pressure."

The inflation caused by over-ambitious financial policies, what's more, was said to ignite further inflation: workers, wanting to "catch up" with inflation and expecting that prices would continue to rise, insisted on big wage increases that raised costs of production and thereby gave the price level another upward push. In Canada critics singled out the federal government's budget deficits for special condemnation. They were declared to be indicators of poor economic management and, as well, a primary cause of the inflation problem; furthermore, their continuation would endanger the country's very financial solvency.

The remedy proposed for both the inflation problem and the deficit menace was simple and straightforward. Experts said government spending would have to be sharply limited, both to curb inflationary pressure and to bring down the federal deficit; taxes would have to be kept high to restrict the public's spending power and because any reduction of government revenue would entail increase in the deficit. The country's money supply would have to be tightly curbed so that people simply wouldn't have the money with which to pay higher prices.

The advocates of these measures acknowledged that tight limitations on spending would cause many people to lose their jobs. The unemployment of hundreds of thousands of persons was an unfortunate but unavoidable cost that would have to be borne, in their view, if inflation was to be fought successfully. The high rate of unemployment would not last forever. Success in the battle against inflation, achieved by monetary and fiscal restraints, would produce a change in labour's expectations. Once the rate of inflation subsided, workers would expect the lower rate to continue and would be content with modest, non-inflationary wage increases.

According to one view, once workers became conditioned to demand only small pay increases, the economy could be safely stimulated to generate jobs for the unemployed. Credit could be eased; taxes could be lowered; government spending could be increased. Thanks to workers' lowered expectations, the additional spending would not rekindle inflation; it would just create more jobs. According to another view, however, expressed by Jean Chrétien, John Crosbie, and Allan MacEachen during their respective tenures of the finance ministry, it would never be appropriate for the government to apply stimuli to the economy to achieve full employment; such measures could only produce inflation. For full employment Canada would have to await an eventual U.S. recovery that would carry the Canadian economy upward along with it.

It is widely considered to be absolutely necessary to maintain firmly the monetary and fiscal restraints until inflation is "squeezed out" of the economy, despite the admittedly heavy cost of unemployment for a large number of people. Determined adherence to a policy of restraint will make possible achievement of the golden goal of long-run price stability combined with full employment. For short-term pain there will be long-term gain, in the phrase coined by John Crosbie. Abandonment of the restraint program and application of stimuli instead to reduce the unemployment problem would produce only a temporary benefit, experts warn, and the costs of those stimuli would bring a further increase in the government's already oppressive burden of debt and interest payments on debt.

This is the "establishment" view of the inflation problem that Canada has been experiencing since the 1960s. It is the view that has been expressed by leading academic economists in learned journals and in the media; it is the view propounded by journalistic commentators on public affairs and by business leaders in public addresses and representations to government.

The view is not monolithic. There are differences of opinion as to what types of restraint measure are most appropriate. The business community urges cuts in government spending to curb inflation and reduce the deficit and, as well, to desirably curtail the role played by the government in the economy. Public administrators and a considerable number of academics favour a policy of tax increases to curb inflation and reduce the deficit, since this would not require the government to curtail its activities and services. Financial experts and a prominent group of academics favour monetary restraint along with reduction in government spending to curb inflation and reduce the deficit. A sufficient degree of monetary restraint, they urge, would make inflation impossible by limiting the total spending power of the country to an amount that was non-inflationary. What's more, since the authorities would control only the aggregate of spending, it would be market forces, not a collection of politicians and bureaucrats, that would decide how the available money was to be spent.

There is division of opinion, too, as to how vigorously restraint measures should be applied. Some people, advocating a "cold turkey" treatment, urge drastic measures that would in short order end the

problems of inflation and budget deficits: very large cuts in government spending, sharp increases in taxation, major reductions in the
money supply. They recognize that such measures would have severely disruptive effects but insist that this would only be temporary;
such a cure would prove to be more effective and, overall, less painful
than a long drawn-out series of moderately restrictive measures.
Thus the C.D. Howe Institute, a leading Canadian think tank, urged
in 1985 that the government immediately slash the deficit from $35
billion to $20 billion. Business leaders, in contrast, suggest that a
cut of $7 billion to $8 billion would be appropriate. Other people,
while acknowledging the desirability of a large reduction in the
deficit, nevertheless counsel that it be achieved more gradually. Prime
Minister Mulroney has promised only that the government will
"beaver away" at the deficit, meaning presumably that it will undertake a long series of small reductions rather than large, dramatic
slashes.

   While politicians of all stripes generally accept the establishment view that inflation is caused by excessive spending, there are
notable differences in the anti-inflation strategies they have applied
while actually in office. The inflation rate surged to worrisome levels
in the late 1960s, when the Liberals were in power in Ottawa, and
they applied restraints on government spending and increases in
taxation, as called for by the conventional wisdom. In addition, they
undertook a series of initiatives (described in Chapter 3) intended to
hold down the size of wage and profit increases. The Conservatives,
during their brief tenure of office in 1979 and since they regained
office in 1984, have made no attempt to influence wage rates and
profit margins directly, since this would be contrary to their ideological commitment to non-intervention by government in the
marketplace.

   Members of all political parties have expressed concern about
the ballooning of the federal deficit since 1975. Conservatives vehemently condemn them; since the deficits swelled to huge proportions under a previous Liberal administration, they are juicy targets
for partisan political criticism. As well, they reflect what Conservatives genuinely regard as a grossly excessive increase in the size of
government and the range of its activities, and a threat to the financial
stability of the country.

   The stance actually adopted by the government towards the
budget deficit issue does not, however, depend solely on which party

is in office; it depends as well on the personal convictions of the individual who is minister of finance. Thus Conservative John Crosbie, who held the position in 1979, and Conservative Michael Wilson, who took it on in 1984, have both actively attempted to reduce the size of the deficit. So did Liberal Allan MacEachen, minister of finance from 1980 to 1982. Liberal Jean Chrétien did not attempt to reduce the deficit but firmly opposed measures of economic stimulation that might have increased it. Liberal Marc Lalonde took a more relaxed view of the deficit, assuring the Canadian people that it didn't portend catastrophe and that the government would have no difficulty paying the interest charges on its mounting debt. To deal with a seriously worsened unemployment problem, he undertook a modest program of economic stimulation that would likely involve at least a temporary increase in the size of the deficit.

The Bank of Canada, meanwhile, has maintained generally restrictive monetary policies that on occasion cause sharp increases in interest rates. These increases in interest rates are invariably denounced by the Opposition and defended by the party in power – which itself denounced similar increases in the past when it was the Opposition.

Every finance minister who has tried to reduce the deficit has relied primarily on reductions in government spending rather than increases in taxation. For government spending is in any case under heavy attack. In the view of a great many politicians, pundits, and business leaders, it has no redeeming features. It provides few jobs and furnishes no useful output. It is a burden on the taxpayers and the major cause of inflation. Businesses particularly denounce the government's "waste and extravagance," its "bloated bureaucracy," its welfare programs that "cost more than the country could afford," and they demand that it "cut out the fat," "live within its means," "tighten its belt."

Prime Minister Trudeau represented this view, too, in less colourful language, with his announcement in August 1978 that to stimulate the economy the federal government would cut its spending by $2.5 billion. As a further stimulant he would clamp down on the federal civil service, requiring public employees to work much harder and not increasing their number. In a manner that he left unexplained, these measures, he declared, would increase the number of jobs available to Canadians. A member of his cabinet later expressed the same point of view. In 1983 John Roberts, then minister of employment and immigration, promised that the government would restrain its spending, in order not to impede the economic recovery that was then proceeding.

THREE

Bitter Pills

C'est magnifique mais ce n'est pas la guerre.
  GENERAL PIERRE BOSQUET, on the charge of the Light Brigade

The Canadian economy did very well in the two decades following World War II, but its performance deteriorated thereafter. New situations and problems arose; to deal with them the government applied policies based on traditional economic doctrines that had been developed in past times, in other countries, in very different circumstances.

Prices rose quite sharply in the first half-dozen years after the end of World War II, but it was generally recognized that the increases were the consequence of extraordinary developments. The inflation that occurred in 1947 and 1948 clearly resulted from the lifting of the wartime price, wage, and profit controls, and the increase of 1951 was obviously caused by the outbreak of the Korean War in the previous year. The persistence of inflation for over a decade afterwards, however, when there were no extraordinary developments to occasion it, caused concern, even though the rate averaged only about 2 per cent. That concern intensified when the inflation rate rose to 3.7 per cent in 1966, and the authorities applied restrictive policies to bring it down from this unacceptably high level.

The measures adopted reflected, for the most part, the Keynesian-monetarist view that inflation was caused by excessive spending, which was fuelled by excessive increase in the country's money supply. The federal government limited its own spending and introduced tax increases to reduce spending by everyone else. In 1967 it raised the federal sales tax from 11 to 12 per cent in order to leave the public with less money, and the next year Parliament legislated a 3-per-cent surcharge on all personal and corporate income, which was levied for three years.

Another change in the income tax was intended to curtail a specific form of spending. A large number of commercial buildings were being erected at this time in the large cities of Ontario, Alberta, and British Columbia, and the authorities considered this construction to be a large factor in the country's inflation problem. Building contractors in these cities had substantially raised their rates of pay in order to obtain all the workers they needed. Contractors elsewhere in the country had to raise their rates of pay correspondingly in order to keep their employees, so the inflation of pay spread nationwide. To curb this particular inflationary pressure, a new income tax provision, introduced in 1969, imposed a financial penalty on developers who put up commercial buildings in any one of the designated cities.

To supplement the anti-inflationary measures already being applied in the late 1960s, the government tried something new. In 1969 it set up the Prices and Incomes Commission, closely modelled on a British body created a few years previously. The commission was given the power to review proposed price increases but not the power to prevent them; if it considered a proposed price increase excessive, it could only appeal to the seller not to go ahead with it. The government hoped that the prospect of adverse publicity would induce firms to heed such appeals.

The chairman of the commission urged labour to limit its demands for wage increases to a "guideline" figure of 6 per cent and appealed to businesses to raise their prices by less than cost increases. The federal and provincial governments agreed to limit the pay increases they gave to their respective employees to the guideline figure, promised not to increase their taxation and spending, and undertook not to buy from any firms that defied a commission request not to raise prices.

In response to the commission's appeal, leading members of the Canadian business community pledged their firms to hold down profit margins. Labour leaders, however, refused to accept the principle of a "guideline" limitation on pay increases. Postal workers demanded a higher increase in 1970 and went on strike when the government refused to give them more than the guideline. The lack of mail delivery caused serious disruption and hardship; finally, after the strike had gone on for forty-nine days, the government gave postal workers a pay increase of 7 per cent. A lengthy strike by General Motors employees that year was also settled only when the firm agreed to pay increases in excess of the guideline. The commission thereupon announced that the guideline policy would be formally ended as of December 31, 1970, and it was itself dissolved soon afterwards.

A new concern materialized in 1971, in the form of a rise in the unemployment rate to 6.4 per cent, a disturbing figure in light of past experience; over the previous two decades the rate had averaged 4.6 per cent, and in only three years had it been above 6 per cent. Henceforth, while the government still considered inflation to be the country's foremost economic problem, attempts to deal with it had to be tempered by concern about possible aggravation of the unemployment problem. So the federal budget of 1971 included a number of measures designed to generate jobs: the rates of personal and corporate income taxes were slightly reduced; loans were made on favourable terms to municipalities for labour-intensive public works projects; old age pensions were slightly increased; programs were instituted to create summer jobs for students and winter jobs for others. The scale of all these measures was small, however, since inflation was still regarded as the country's most threatening economic problem; it was accepted that some worsening of the unemployment problem would have to be endured if the more serious menace was to be effectively dealt with. Prime Minister Trudeau indicated his priorities by the declaration that he was determined to "wrestle inflation to the ground," even if the consequence was an unemployment rate in excess of 6 per cent.

John Turner, then the minister of finance, introduced a mildly expansionary budget in 1973, its most notable feature being the indexation of the personal income tax exemption. The object of indexation was to ensure that the government didn't profit from inflation, at the taxpayer's expense. The personal exemption for each taxpayer was $1,600 at the time; if inflation occurred, the real value of this exemption would be reduced. Indexation provided that the exemption be increased each year by the current inflation rate, thereby maintaining its value in real terms.

Two years later, both inflation and unemployment had worsened, and stronger measures were applied. In June 1975 Turner brought down a budget that featured restrictions on spending to contain inflation, together with increases allocated to job generation programs, intended to ease the current unemployment problem. It soon became evident, however, that this budget, as restrictive as political realities allowed, would not restrain the powerful inflationary pressures that had developed in the country.

So in October 1975, Prime Minister Trudeau announced a new anti-inflation program that featured controls over wages and profits together with intensification of fiscal and monetary restraints. The program, to be in effect till the end of 1978, was designed to bring the inflation rate down gradually. Designated categories of workers, notably civil servants and the employees of large firms, totalling about half the country's labour force, would be subject to the jurisdiction of the Anti-Inflation Board.

For the first year of the program the board announced a "guideline" figure of 12 per cent, which had this significance: if a union negotiated a new contract with an employer that provided for a pay increase of more than 12 per cent, the contract had to be referred to the board. The board could let the contract stand, or it could "roll back" the pay increase to whatever figure it saw fit, the governing consideration being the "historic relationship" between the pay of the workers involved and the pay of other workers with which some "long-term relationship" existed. A negotiated pay increase of less than 12 per cent did not have to be referred to the board; it would go through without question. The guideline figure would decline in stages to 8 per cent.

Although only about half of the country's workers were made subject to these regulations, there was a strong likelihood that the regulations would effectively extend to all. Prime Minister Trudeau expressed the hope that the workers who were not required to comply with them would voluntarily do so. In any case, since the workers not covered by the legislation were in smaller, less visible units and had weaker bargaining power, it was unlikely that they would be able to win gains larger than those allowed to the workers who were subject to the controls.

Profit margins were also limited. If a firm achieved an increase in its profit for the year with no increase in sales but simply because it had a wider profit margin, it would be required to return the excess to its customers.

Trade union leaders furiously opposed the controls over wages on the grounds that they denied the fundamental freedom of workers to negotiate contracts with their employers. Labour in Canada staged a national "Day of Protest" in 1976, with demonstrations in a number of cities, to show its opposition to wage controls. The country's business managers, while less vocal and demonstrative, angrily opposed the control over profits as unwarranted interference by the government in the operations of the marketplace. As well, they were thoroughly exasperated by the requirement that they fill out innumerable detailed reports, a task that took an enormous amount of time and effort. In light of the hostility expressed by both labour and the business community, the government ended the program about eight months early.

The controls over wages and profits were only part of the anti-inflation program announced by Trudeau in October 1975. In addition, there were to be fiscal and monetary restraints: the government would curb its spending and the Bank of Canada would tighten credit conditions in the country. The governor of the Bank, Gerald Bouey, announced in November that the Bank would act to reduce the growth rate of the national money supply from its double-digit magnitude to a level close to the economy's real growth rate of 2 to 3 per cent. Since a sudden, large reduction could have seriously disruptive effects on the economy, Bouey added that the reduction would be carried out in stages, over a period of years. What's more, since it would really be impossible to achieve exactly any projected figure, the Bank would take a range of figures as its target. Accordingly, in 1975 it announced a target range of 10 to 15 per cent for that year's growth rate of the money supply; in the next half-dozen years, it announced a series of further reductions. By 1981 the target growth rate of the money supply was down to the 4- to 8-per-cent range. This program of monetary restraint was reflected in developments in financial markets: the prime interest rate soared to a peak of 22.75 per cent in 1981 and mortgage interest rates rose to over 21 per cent; federal government bond issues of 1981 paid an average of over 15 per cent interest.

In 1982 the Bank of Canada announced that it would no longer attempt to achieve specific monetary targets, because it had become impossible to determine just how big the country's money supply was at any given time. When it had undertaken its new policy of restraint in 1975 the Bank had assumed the country's money supply to consist of the currency in circulation plus the demand deposits in banks upon which cheques could be written. It had not included savings deposits upon which cheques could not be written and on which interest was paid – calculated typically on the minimum monthly balance. However, once computerization made it possible, the chartered banks began offering savings accounts on which interest was calculated on a daily basis. Accordingly, a great many people and business firms shifted *all* their bank deposits to these accounts, with the result that funds that constituted savings and funds that constituted means of payment were now lumped together in one type of account and could not be distinguished from each other. The widespread use of credit cards created another problem for anyone attempting to determine the size of the national money supply, for here was a new means of payment whose size was virtually incalculable.

While acknowledging that a policy of specifically designated growth rates for the money supply was not feasible, Bouey gave assurance that the Bank of Canada would continue to exercise restraint; it would continue to prevent inflationary increases in the money supply. And in fact while interest rates in Canada came down from the record levels of 1981, they continued in the 1980s to be high by historic standards, about twice as high as they had been before 1966, when the ceiling was removed.

While adhering to its program of reduction of the growth rate of the national money supply, the Bank of Canada encountered inflationary pressure from another source. The foreign exchange rate of the Canadian dollar was heading downward; that decline was aggravating the country's inflation problem by raising the prices Canadians had to pay for imported goods. Even when foreigners were charging the same price in their own currency for a product, it now took more Canadian dollars to pay that same amount of foreign currency. Since about one-quarter of everything sold in Canada is imported, every one-cent drop in the Canadian dollar's foreign exchange rate raised the cost of living in Canada by about one-quarter of one per cent.

To prevent the dollar from dropping, it was necessary to deter outflows of funds from Canada that would weaken it and to attract inflows of foreign funds that would strengthen it. That meant keeping interest rates in Canada equal to or above those of the U.S.; otherwise Canadians would send their savings to the U.S. and no Americans – or anyone else, for that matter – would send their money here. If interest rates rose in the U.S. it would be necessary, therefore, for interest rates in Canada to rise correspondingly. In fact the U.S. monetary authorities, determined to throttle inflation, very tightly restricted the growth of the country's money supply, thereby causing a wild escalation of interest rates. The need to prevent decline in the foreign exchange rate of the Canadian dollar thus provided the Bank of Canada with another reason for allowing interest rates to rise to unprecedented levels above 20 per cent.

From 1979 to 1982 the inflation rate averaged about 11 per cent, a level that, in the view of a great many people, threatened disaster for the national economy. Meanwhile, concern grew about another problem. Since 1975 the federal government had incurred budget deficits that were absolutely unprecedented in size and swiftly ballooned to frightening proportions. Whereas previously, in peacetime, there had been a rough balance between budget deficits and surpluses, and the largest deficit ever incurred had been about $1 billion, in 1975 the deficit was over $5 billion, and in the next half-dozen years it averaged over $11 billion.

Grave concern was expressed at the rapid escalation of the federal government's debt and the accompanying burden of interest charges. There was widespread agreement that the government ought to give the highest priority to reduction of its deficits. Commentators warned that the federal deficit was a "ticking time bomb" that threatened financial catastrophe in the future and in the meantime was responsible for inflation, unemployment, and high interest rates. When, in 1978, the Economic Council of Canada advocated that the government spend $2 billion to generate jobs, the minister of finance, Jean Chrétien, dismissed the proposal as irresponsible since it would increase the deficit. The budget proposed in 1979 by John Crosbie, minister of finance in the short-lived Clark government, featured expenditure reductions and tax increases that were expected to reduce the deficit. The budget introduced in 1981 by Allan MacEachen was designed to reduce the deficit from $13 billion to $10 billion, by a combination of spending cuts and tax increases.

To hold down its own expenditures, and as an anti-inflation measure, the government in 1982 introduced the "6 and 5" program, under which the pay increases of federal employees were limited to 6 per cent in the current year and 5 per cent in the following year. The government urged provincial administrations – and employers generally – to abide by these figures, and many did. Provincial governments and many private employers gave their employees increases that were in fairly close accord with the federal figures. Meanwhile, the unemployment rate in Canada soared from 7.5 per cent in 1981 to 11.0 per cent in 1982; a good many commentators claimed, with considerable justification, that heavy unemployment was the main reason for the sharp decline that occurred in the magnitude of wage increases.

Marc Lalonde, named minister of finance in 1982, was less concerned than his predecessors about the deficit and assured the country that the government would have no difficulty in meeting the interest obligations on its already accumulated debt. To deal with the suddenly expanded problem of unemployment, he introduced a $1-billion program of job generation in 1982, estimating that this would create 60,000 jobs. The following year he announced a three-year job generation program under which a total of $4.8 billion would be spent. The funds for both these programs were to be obtained without increase in the federal deficit: the $1 billion was obtained through transfer from other programs; the $4.8 billion was to be recouped by a 1-per-cent increase in the sales tax, beginning in 1984. The scale of these programs was, in any case, modest. They were expected to generate 60,000 to 100,000 jobs a year – when the number of unemployed in the country was about 1.5 million.

Following the victory of the Conservative party in the federal election of 1984, Brian Mulroney became prime minister and appointed Michael Wilson as his minister of finance. Both men have repeatedly declared the federal deficit to be the country's foremost economic problem. In his first two budgets, Wilson has instituted a number of spending cuts and tax increases, designed to narrow the gap between the federal government's expenditures and revenues. Mulroney, in a confrontation with provincial premiers, firmly adhered to the stand that the federal government must reduce the growth rate of its grants to provinces to a level below the figure promised by the previous Liberal administration.

The cuts in government spending announced by Mulroney and Wilson reflect not just a desire to reduce the federal budget but commitment to the ideological view that the government should play a smaller role in the economy. A Conservative task force has examined the government's operations and concluded that it is performing many functions that are unnecessary or would be better handled by private enterprise. Spending cuts serve the dual purpose of reducing the deficit and "streamlining" the government's operations – making them more cost-effective, eliminating waste and duplication, ending activities that the government ought not to be engaged in. Reduction of the deficit would instil a new confidence in the business community that would encourage desirable investment and expansion. To reduce unemployment, the government is relying not on job generation schemes but on training programs that will qualify unemployed persons for jobs generated by private-sector expansion.

FOUR

Divergent Second Opinion

And, oftentimes, to win us to our harm,
The instruments of darkness tell us truths;
Win us with honest trifles, to betray's
In deepest consequence.
    SHAKESPEARE, Macbeth

The economic difficulties that emerged in Canada in the 1960s derived from a unique combination of historic developments. Technology advanced rapidly on many fronts; Far Eastern nations gained a large share of the world market for industrial products; momentous changes occurred in social attitudes. Proper diagnosis and treatment of Canada's economic problems required recognition of the fact that they were produced and shaped by these historic changes. Economic analysis and policy showed little such recognition.

A new view of inflation surfaced in the 1960s, not associated with the name of any one individual. It denied that the originating cause of contemporary inflation was excessive spending as the Keynesians claimed, that it was excessive increase in the money supply as the Friedmanites claimed, that it was an insufficiently high level of unemployment as the Phillipists claimed. These might have been the causes of inflation in the past but they were not responsible for the inflation that was going on currently. It was of a new type, derived from a unique combination of major historical developments – World War II, the post-war revolutionary changes in social attitudes, the sweeping advances in technology, the vastly enhanced power of trade unions, the emergence of gigantic business organizations, the enormously enlarged role played by governments in the operation of national economies.

The novelty of the new inflation was attested to by the fact that it was accompanied by high rates of unemployment. In the past an economy that was experiencing inflation operated at feverish tempo, generating an intense demand for labour; employers characteristically wanted to hire more workers than the number available. Now Canada, along with many other countries, was experiencing "stagflation," a combination of high inflation and high unemployment.

An account of the new phenomenon properly begins with the observation that it was the government's enormous spending on the war effort that ended the Great Depression of the 1930s. During the peak war years, 1942 to 1945, government spending for military purposes amounted to more than 30 per cent of the GNP, the equivalent of over $150 billion today. Federal budget deficits averaged 21 per cent of the GNP, the equivalent of deficits today of well over $100 billion. When the war ended, in 1945, the national debt was nearly four times what it had been in 1939; it amounted to 155 per cent of the GNP, the equivalent to a national debt today of about $800 billion. It was these colossal outlays, financed entirely by Canadian taxpayers and Canadian lenders, that obliterated the country's unemployment problem, driving the unemployment rate down from the 22-per-cent figure of 1933 to nearly zero in 1944.

Contrary to the virtually unanimous predictions of experts, the end of the war did not bring financial collapse or even renewal of economic depression; an immense demand now developed for peacetime goods and services. Nor was the new generation impoverished by the burden of debt that the federal government had incurred. The quarter-century from 1946 to 1970 was the most prosperous and stable in Canadian history, with the unemployment rate averaging under 4 per cent, the inflation rate averaging about 3 per cent, the real growth per year averaging over 2 per cent. The generation that came to maturity following the war in fact enjoyed a standard of living far higher than that of any previous generation.

The Canadian public, starved for civilian goods throughout the war and holding ample financial assets in the form of bank balances and war bonds, snapped up whatever retailers put on their shelves and demanded more. Canadian businesses, unable to properly maintain their plant during the Depression for lack of cash and during the war for lack of labour and materials, now scrambled to make up for that neglect. Foreign countries that had been battlefields, unable to provide for themselves because of the destruction they had suffered in wartime, and liberally supplied with U.S. funds by gift and loan, eagerly bought whatever other countries could supply, at first to stay alive and then to rebuild their shattered economies. Canada, with its immense capacity for the production of foodstuffs, minerals, and lumber – and unscathed by war – had a great deal that they needed and exported to them on a huge scale.

With demand strong for their products, employers in practically every type of enterprise eagerly sought workers to help produce the goods they could profitably sell. The discharge of over 500,000 people from the armed forces and the lay-offs of over a million persons from jobs in war industries did not give rise to an unemployment problem. A good many older persons and married women who had worked out of patriotic obligation went quietly back to retirement or to being home-makers. With their departure from the labour force and the buoyant economic conditions, almost all the people who sought jobs were able to find them. The number of unemployed rose only marginally, to 124,000 in 1946, less than a sixth of the 1933 figure; from 1946 to 1949 the unemployment rate reported by trade unions averaged only 2.1 per cent.

The task of reconstruction was largely completed within half a dozen years of the war's end; Europe fully recovered its pre-war capability by 1951. However, a number of historic developments during the next two decades kept in high gear the economies of the Western world. Private entrepreneurs and public authorities in many lands built the immense and diversified plant that would enable the populations of Western countries to enjoy a new and affluent life-style, characterized by highly mechanized agriculture and industry, near-universal ownership of automobiles and a wide array of electrical appliances, roomy housing in suburbias and exurbias, frequent holiday trips by automobile and aircraft for a large proportion of national populations.

Numberless factories were built to produce the thousands of aircraft, the millions of tractors, automobiles, and appliances; steel mills and other metal-processing plants were built to supply the factories with the materials they needed; mines were dug in resource-endowed countries to obtain the iron, nickel, copper, lead, zinc, and other ores that were the raw materials of the processing plants. To serve travellers, governments built highways, bridges, airfields, and air terminals; private enterprise built hotels, motels, restaurants, and places of entertainment. To provide the fuel required by mechanical vehicles, private enterprise drilled oil wells and built refineries and pipelines. Governments and private enterprise built electricity generating stations to provide the energy needed by industry, to light cities, to power appliances.

Military conflict provided additional economic stimulus, especially to the U.S. The Korean War (1950–53) brought strong demand for the products of armament industries and indirectly, therefore, for the host of materials required in their production. The Vietnam War, which extended over much of the 1960s, generated corresponding demand that had widespread stimulative effect.

Centres of industrial power outside the U.S. expanded substantially in the post-war era, challenging that country's long-standing industrial domination. Formation of the European Economic Community in 1957 prompted investment in gigantic plants that became economically feasible once Europe constituted itself into a single enormous market. Japan developed an industrial complex that rivalled that of the U.S. in size and range of capability. Smaller countries like Korea and Taiwan and cities like Singapore and Hong Kong became world-scale manufacturers of industrial products, many of which incorporated highly advanced technology.

The economic development that occurred in Canada in the 1950s and 1960s was an integral part of this worldwide advance. The industrial expansion going on in other countries required raw materials that Canada provided: mines were dug here to extract ores and smelters and refineries were built to process those ores; trees were felled and mills built to convert logs into lumber and paper; railways, docks, and waterways were improved in order to convey materials efficiently to their markets. Exploration for oil in western Canada, the drilling of wells, the construction of pipelines and refineries furnished the fuel required to power Canada's tractors, automobiles, railways, and airlines, to conveniently heat its buildings. Among the mega-projects of the time were the Iron Ore Company's mine at Schefferville, with its associated railway to Sept-Îles, the Alcan project in northern British Columbia, and the St. Lawrence Seaway.

Some of the expansion of industrial capacity was carried out in Canada – but only a relatively small part. Expansion occurred of the industries in which Canada had some entrepreneurial or geographic advantage or those to which government gave some form of special assistance. But these were relatively few; Canada imported most of the manufactured products required by the new lifestyle.

Canada's urban population increased rapidly in the 1950s and 1960s, because of high levels of immigration, an exodus from farms that was brought on by agricultural mechanization, and a baby boom that followed the record number of marriages in the early post-war years. A great amount of housing and the service establishments required by the new urban and suburban populations were constructed, with strong support from the federal government. As they did elsewhere in the world, public authorities built transportation networks, public utilities, schools, and hospitals; private enterprise built the commercial establishments.

By the 1970s the pace of economic activity throughout much of the industrialized world was slackening. The task of reconstructing what had been damaged or destroyed during the war had been completed. Most of the present industrial structure of Europe had been put in place. So had many of the public works and facilities and private business establishments required by the new lifestyles. The Vietnam War was coming to an end. The effects of economic slowdown were compounded by market shifts. Technological advance produced substitutes for traditional materials such as copper; the smaller, lighter cars demanded by purchasers – and insisted on by governments – required less steel and therefore reduced the need for iron ore. The world needed less of Canada's industrial raw materials; the problem of a diminished world market was aggravated for Canada by the rising competition of new sources of supply in Africa and South America.

Canada's manufacturing industries suffered, too, from increasing competition. Firms in Japan, Korea, Hong Kong, Singapore, and Taiwan turned out rapidly growing quantities of sophisticated goods such as vehicles, machinery, and electronic products. Those same countries, together with low-income, developing countries the world over, produced ever-larger quantities of unsophisticated products such as cheap clothing and footwear.

In Canada – outside of Alberta, where activity exploded in response to soaring oil and gas prices – there were few huge developmental projects of the type that had galvanized the economy in the 1950s and 1960s. Construction activity tended downward for yet another reason: the rate of urban population growth slackened as immigration declined, the baby boom slowed, and the exodus from farms virtually ended. Industrial expansion did not end abruptly. Private enterprise continued to develop new consumer products and new production technologies, but these did not require industrial construction on the massive scale of previous decades. Governments continued to build public facilities and public works, but such construction was generally on a smaller scale, and the projects were of a lower order of priority.

This historic sequence was like the experience of an agricultural dynasty. The first generation is fully occupied with activities that are absolutely essential: clearing the land, building a house and barn. These primary tasks do not have to be performed again; a succeeding generation can achieve, with less effort, the same production as did the pioneers – thanks to the work done and the legacy left by those pioneers. If a following generation is content to have the same level of output, then it can have more leisure time than the pioneers. If the members of a later generation want to be just as fully occupied as their forbears, they will have to spend a good deal of their time on projects that are not as important as those carried out by the pioneers; they will spend much of their time making living arrangements more convenient, surroundings more attractive, their lifestyle more interesting.

While developmental activity was generally slower in the 1970s than it had been in the 1950s and 1960s, inflation rates were higher, for a number of reasons. Arab oil-exporting nations raised the price of a barrel of oil fivefold in 1973, to punish the Western world for its support of Israel in the Arab–Israeli conflict. They added further increases in the next few years, so that by 1980 the price of a barrel of oil was about fifteen times what it had been in 1972. In a world that had come to depend on oil to fuel vehicles, generate electrical power, and heat buildings, the cost of living and the cost of practically every type of production rose sharply.

At the same time, the prices of major foods soared. The U.S.S.R. harvested a disastrously poor crop in 1972 and bought large amounts of wheat in the U.S. to meet its needs. Its purchases took so large a proportion of American stocks that shortages loomed in the U.S. The price of wheat trebled in the next two years, causing sharp increases in the price of bread and of all foods derived from animals that were fed on grain – meats, poultry, dairy products. The increase in the cost of living that stemmed from increases in oil and food prices prompted workers everywhere to insist on corresponding wage increases, giving production costs another upward boost.

Throughout the industrialized world the new generation of workers was very different in its composition, attitudes, and organization from workers of times past. Workers had higher aspirations than ever before, together with greater capacity to achieve them. In exercising that capacity they applied strong upward pressure on wage rates, and therefore on production costs and price levels.

In European countries revolutionary change in educational arrangements after World War II played a large role in reshaping worker attitudes. No longer were working-class children taught only the rudiments, in free public schools that they alone attended. Now rich and poor children alike went to the same state-supported schools, where they received the same instruction and were exposed to the same influences. While the virtual elimination of private, fee-paying schools did not eliminate all disparities, the effects of the educational rearrangement were profound. Far more working-class children acquired education that enabled them to become professionals, executives, and political leaders. Those who remained in the working class had higher self-esteem; no longer was it impressed on them at school that they were inferior people who would have to patiently accept low social status and income.

In Canada and the U.S. too, the educational gap between wage workers and other social classes was narrowed after World War II, but by a completely different set of developments. In both countries educational opportunity had been almost equally available to all, even in the nineteenth century. Both countries, however, had received in the first decade or so of the twentieth century huge numbers of immigrants from southern and eastern Europe. A large proportion of the newcomers were teenagers and young adults who had received the barest minimum of education, or none at all, in their countries of origin. For the next few decades, until retirement and death took their toll, they constituted a substantial element of the labour force in Canada and the U.S.

In both countries during this time there was another large category of persons with limited education. These were people who had grown up in rural areas where schooling arrangements were scant and primitive. Following World War II this category of person virtually disappeared, as mechanization peacefully decimated farm populations and the new mobility conferred by automotive vehicles and close-meshed road networks made it possible to provide rural children with almost the same standard of education as was being provided to urban children.

By the 1960s the Canadian labour force no longer included the same large proportion of workers with limited education who deferentially accepted inferior social status and lower pay as their appropriate lot. The majority of immigrants who came to Canada after

World War II were not unlettered peasants and labourers like the majority of newcomers in the pre–World War I era. Instead, immigrants were mostly quite well educated, qualified for skilled, clerical, and managerial employments. (The U.S., in contrast to Canada, continued to have in its labour force large low-status elements – blacks and Hispanics.)

Television, almost universally available in the Western world by the 1960s, contributed powerfully to homogenization of the attitudes and aspiration levels of national populations. The identical entertainments, news, and views were brought to every household; the same dazzling cornucopia of commercial products was displayed to absolutely everyone; cleverly conceived advertising impressed equally on all how their lives would be enriched by the possession of those products.

Favourable legislation in both Canada and the U.S. conferred new rights on trade unions, encouraging their expansion and enabling them to achieve more for their members. The historic Wagner Act of 1935 assured U.S. workers of the right to organize themselves into unions of their own choosing, and it required employers to bargain with their representatives in good faith. Exactly the same rights were accorded to Canadian workers by order-in-council during World War II and then by federal and provincial legislation in peacetime. As a result of subsequent enactments, Canadian legislation in fact became relatively more supportive of trade unions. The U.S. Taft-Hartley Act of 1947 imposed curbs on trade unions, and many state legislatures passed "right-to-work" laws that forbade the "closed shop" and the "union shop" – that is, the requirement that membership in a union be a condition of employment. There were no corresponding enactments in Canada. The Public Services Staff Relations Act, passed by Parliament in 1967, gave federal employees the right to organize themselves into unions for the purpose of collective bargaining and permitted them to go on strike to enforce their demands; employees of the U.S. government, on the other hand, were expressly forbidden to strike.

While changes in legislation altered the legal status and powers of trade unions, precedent-setting developments introduced new attitudes and practices in negotiations between employers and trade unions. The landmark agreement of 1950 between General Motors and the United Auto Workers provided that workers should receive an increase in pay every year, so that they too would share in the country's productivity growth. This principle eventually became commonplace, in Canada as well as the U.S. What's more, union negotiators bargained not just for increases that would correspond to productivity growth but for the maximum that could be levered out of employers, in the form of raises in pay, improvements in fringe benefits, and increases in job security. So long as the economy was buoyant, they were typically able to win large gains, as employers were prepared to make substantial concessions in order to avoid or end costly strikes.

Pay raises were often well above productivity increases, pushing up labour costs per unit of output. Employers raised their selling prices to maintain their profit margins. Whenever the cost of living rose, for reasons such as an increase in food prices caused by a poor harvest, workers, to maintain their real incomes, insistently demanded corresponding increases in pay. Once an increase was granted, union representatives, in negotiating the next contract, pressed determinedly for an increase of at least the same size, so that large pay raises – and therefore inflation – tended to be perpetuated.

With employers forbidden to interfere with attempts at unionization by their workers and obliged to negotiate in good faith with their representatives, unions were able to recruit many more members and to achieve much more for them. A much larger proportion of the labour force became unionized – an even larger proportion in Canada than in the U.S.; correspondingly, more pay rates were set in negotiations between employers and union representatives who determinedly applied the bargaining power conferred by collective action.

In both Canada and the U.S. the composition and outlook of the national labour force altered significantly over time. Decline steadily occurred in the number of workers who had been adults during the 1930s and, having then come to regard a state of depression as normal, were apprehensive in the 1950s and 1960s that the current prosperity was only a bubble that would soon burst. The proportion of the labour force grew ever larger of persons who knew only a state of full employment and who had no experience of times when workers counted themselves fortunate just to have jobs and cuts in pay were as likely as increases.

The stronger legal status of trade unions and their greatly increased membership were accompanied by a far higher degree of public acceptance of their activities. There were now far fewer of the savage conflicts between strikers and strike-breakers that had previously been commonplace. The general public accepted with resignation and relatively mild resentment the inconvenience caused by strikes. There were fewer instances of dogged refusal by employers to make any concessions to unions. Many employers made no attempt to recruit replacements for employees who were on strike. The milder resistance offered to strikes made them less dangerous to undertake, more likely to succeed. What's more, the higher pay earned by workers enabled them to accumulate larger savings; their unions were able to build up bigger strike funds. They were therefore better able to cope with lack of earnings during a strike and were less likely to be forced by privation to capitulate.

Upward pressure on wage rates in Canada acquired its own unique elements in the 1960s. Quebec trade unions, hitherto especially docile, became especially militant, reflecting the province's new nationalistic mood and the political and social overtones involved in contract negotiations between francophone workers and anglophone employers. In 1966, Montreal construction workers demanded a 30-per-cent wage raise over the next three years, a far greater increase than had been customary: in the previous fifteen years the average annual increase in wage rates in Canada had been 4 per cent. Since a strike by construction workers would jeopardize timely completion of the buildings being erected for the world exposition to be held in 1967, Canada's centennial year, the demand was granted. Also in 1966, Montreal longshoremen demanded an increase even larger than that given to the city's construction workers; after a strike that paralysed the port for thirty-nine days, they were given an increase of 30 per cent over two years. In the next few years federal civil servants, militantly applying the bargaining power conferred on them by the Public Services Staff Relations Act of 1967, won big pay increases.

The large gains of Quebec workers did not remain unique to them; workers in the rest of the country adopted as their goals the levels of pay increase achieved by Quebeckers. The pay raises won by federal employees also had "demonstration effects," as private-sector employees demanded increases comparable to those given to civil servants. Throughout the country and in all industries the norm of pay increases rose sharply; a much higher level of wage increases was the major cause of the acceleration that occurred in Canada's inflation rate in the 1970s.

A political development of 1974 added to the inflationary pressure already being felt in Canada because of the previous year's rise in oil and food prices. Members of Parliament were still being paid at a rate that had been set years before, and their real incomes had been much reduced by the recent inflation. The federal government appointed a committee of eminent businesspeople to consider the issue of MPs' pay and make appropriate recommendations. The committee recommended that the parliamentary indemnity be increased by 50 per cent, to allow for the inflation that had occurred since the amount had last been set and the inflation that presumably would occur until it was changed again.

Parliament approved the increase, with only one member, Stanley Knowles, expressing objection. The fact that members of Parliament were voting themselves a 50-per-cent pay increase raised a storm of protest. (In deference to that reaction, Parliament voted itself not a 50-per-cent increase but two smaller increases, one of 33 per cent and the other of 17 per cent.) Taking their cue from the country's legislators, unions sharply escalated their pay demands. Postal workers, in negotiations for a new contract, began with a demand for an increase of 71 per cent, subsequently moderating it to 51 per cent, a figure that reflected their vehement claim to deserve more than members of Parliament. The average wage increase in new contracts negotiated in the first six months of 1975 was over 20 per cent, threatening sharp escalation of the country's inflation rate and impelling the government to introduce its program of wage and profit controls.

In both Canada and the U.S., workers improved their lot in the 1960s and 1970s not only through increases in pay but through the achievement of new programs of social assistance and improvement of programs already in effect. Applying the political power they possessed as citizens of democracies, they impelled legislatures to institute and improve publicly financed programs that were of special benefit to persons in the lower income brackets—pensions, family allowances, publicly funded health care, unemployment insurance. Outlays on these programs swelled to very large proportions in both Canada and the U.S. By providing income to persons who had not performed productive services in return, these programs contributed to the upward pressure on prices.

The inflation that Canada has experienced since the 1960s has been primarily of the cost-push variety and, in overwhelming degree,

Canadian-made. External developments, even the wild escalation of world oil prices in the 1970s, account for only a small part of the 250-per-cent rise that has occurred in the Canadian price level since 1966. Trade unions, with memberships larger and more determined, leaders more experienced and aided by supportive legislation, have been able to insist on wage increases well in excess of productivity gains. Businesses with market power have broadened their profit margins. Every increase in wages or profits in excess of productivity growth has raised production costs, requiring an increase in selling prices.

Inflation begat more inflation in the 1970s. Increases in pay needed to "keep up with inflation" raised production costs again, requiring further increases in prices. With annual pay increases of about 12 per cent while the country's real output was growing by about 2 per cent, an inflation rate around 10 per cent became a settled feature of the Canadian economy. It is only since the average of pay increases declined to about 5 per cent, in 1983, that the inflation rate has declined sharply.

While inflation is being caused primarily by increases in cost of production, the government has applied remedial policies based on the Keynesian-monetarist doctrine that inflation is always caused by excessive spending – that it is always of the demand-pull variety. Anti-inflation strategy has emphasized holding government spending to the lowest level that political realities allow, holding down private-sector spending by the highest taxation that is acceptable to the electorate, raising interest rates to levels that deter borrowing.

These measures were first applied to an economy whose pace had already begun to slacken. By about 1970 the post-war boom was drawing to a close. If the economic pace of the 1950s and 1960s was to be maintained, stimulants should have been applied; restraints have been imposed instead for their presumed anti-inflationary effect and, in the case of fiscal restraints, to keep down the federal budget deficit.

The primary effect of these measures has been to cause unemployment; they have had mixed effects on the price level. While they have indeed curbed demand, they have also raised a number of costs, especially of borrowing, and prevented increases in market supplies that would have served to push prices downward. They have had significant anti-inflationary effect only when the unemployment they cause is so high that labour is intimidated into moderating its wage demands. Whether the net effect of fiscal and monetary restraints has been to raise or lower the inflation rate is unclear. The average inflation rate in the two decades during which these restraints have been applied has been considerably higher than the average inflation rate during the previous two decades – more than double. It might, of course, have been higher still if the restraints had not been applied. We will never know.

Eruptions at workplaces have reflected the reality that today's generation of workers is different from those of the past. Attempts to maintain traditional arrangements and relationships have roused angry objections. The issue is epitomized by the difficulties that Canada Post has experienced in recent years. Worker hostility towards management has been the major cause of the explosions that have rocked the post office in the last decade.

This hostility has not been in reaction to new rules and procedures that the administration introduced; rather it is due to the administration's failure to change with the times. Postal workers today are different in their outlook and expectations from those of the past, and require different treatment. They have not been getting it.

Many post office jobs are repetitious and monotonous. They offer very little in the way of job satisfaction. Supervisors watch employees closely to ensure that they don't steal and that they abide by detailed rules and regulations. The constant supervision is offensive to self-respect.

These conditions are not new. The work was always repetitious and monotonous; supervisors always kept a close check on employees, closer in the past than now. What is new is the attitude of the workers.

Postal employees of past generations did not complain about their jobs. Having been brought up in a society where authoritarian control by superiors was a fact of life everywhere, they submissively accepted detailed regulation and close supervision. In times when many people had to do heavy manual labour, when roads were built by men with shovels and streets were cleared by men with brooms, a post office job had high status and superior working conditions as well as good pay. Workers were glad to have the job. And if ever employees did have complaints, there was no effective method for expressing them.

In contrast, postal workers of today are people of the 1980s.

They are high school graduates; some have university degrees. They own television sets and drive cars. They have been brought up in a society where all authority is challenged, where the phenomenon of deference to superiors is all but unknown.

Their social status is lower than it used to be, if only because many inferior jobs have disappeared. There is little heavy physical labour done these days; roads are built and streets are swept by workers with machines. A letter-sorter's job does not compare as favourably with other jobs as it used to; its irksome features are less tolerable. What is more, postal workers are now organized into unions that can forcefully represent their dissatisfaction.

The post office administration has been insensitive to the enormous differences between employees of yesteryear and those of today. When it introduces new automatic equipment, it considers only mechanical efficiency; it does not consider how workers would be affected. Employees furiously object to being treated like chattels. With over a million Canadians out of work, they are intensely concerned about the possibility of losing their jobs. They are especially aggrieved that the federal government – which is supposed to uphold the rights and protect the well-being of all citizens – is the employer whom they cannot trust, is totally insensitive to their claims, hammers at their self-respect.

Some pundits have ascribed the post office's problems to militant union leadership. But those leaders are elected by the members. They are elected because workers want leaders who will forcefully represent their views and wants.

The problems of the post office are symptomatic of a broader economic problem. For years now federal policy-makers have ignored a major social reality of our time – a working class that is better informed, better educated, better organized, has higher expectation levels than any previous generation of workers. They have attempted to deal with Canada's inflation problem by applying doctrines derived from the behaviour of English and American workers in the nineteenth century. Small wonder that they have failed.

FIVE

Self-Inflicted Harm

Greatly his foes he dreads, but more his friends.
CHARLES CHURCHILL

Every one of the fiscal and monetary restraints applied against inflation has caused unemployment. To hold down its spending, the
government employs fewer people than it otherwise would do and
buys less from suppliers, obliging them to cut back on staff. Increase
in the personal income tax reduces the public's spending power; sales
are therefore lower and businesses need fewer employees. Increase
in the corporation profit tax takes from firms money that they would
have invested in new plant and reduces the prospective profitability
of such investment; the effect is to reduce employment in the construction industry and related industries. Tightening of the money
supply causes interest rates to rise, deterring investment in new
plant and adding therefore to unemployment in the construction and
construction-related industries.

Canada has lost the immense amount of output that would
have been produced by people had they been working instead of idle.
During the nineteen years before 1966, the year when anti-inflation
measures were first adopted, the unemployment rate in Canada averaged 4.3 per cent. During the nineteen years after 1966, while
policies of fiscal and monetary restraint were being applied, the
unemployment rate averaged 7.5 per cent. The addition of 3.2 per
cent to the unemployment rate meant that the ranks of the unemployed from 1967 to 1985 contained an additional 400,000 persons. The unemployment of those people was responsible for a total
output loss of over $300 billion, in 1985 terms. That is the value of
the goods and services that those persons would have produced if
they had been working instead of unemployed.

Actually, the loss of output has probably been even larger. A
high rate of unemployment is typically accompanied by inferior

productivity on the part of those still working. Many are likely to be working part-time. For want of a steady flow of orders, production runs on an inefficient stop-and-go basis, with workers standing around idle a good deal of the time. Some employees, fearful of being laid off when their present work ends, deliberately go slow in order to make the job last as long as possible. Productivity is likely to be further lowered because a good many people are employed at jobs far below their capabilities. Research physicists drive taxis; engineers sling hamburgers; teachers sell lottery tickets. Productivity improvement is further slowed as workers furiously oppose the introduction of labour-saving equipment; with jobs scarce, they are understandably fearful that if they are displaced by this equipment they will remain unemployed. Possible future gains in productivity are aborted as unemployed workers do not acquire skill and experience that would make them more effective performers in the future; unemployed engineers do not obtain experience, insights, and contacts that would enable them to devise new products, new technology, and improvements in equipment.

Ideas for improving products, for producing more efficiently, do not occur to unemployed people walking the streets or staring despondently into space; they occur to people on the job who see how products could be advantageously modified, how their production could be made more efficient; they occur to people who can discuss ideas with fellow-workers.

High interest rates also abort future productivity gains. By making it costly and dangerous to borrow money, they deter investment in modern equipment that would make industrial plants more productive in the future. Housing is not built that would provide accommodation for future generations. By encouraging borrowing outside the country, high Canadian interest rates increase the debt we owe to foreigners; future generations will be saddled with the obligation to make interest and principal payments to foreigners in foreign currencies. Restrictive fiscal policy has a similar adverse effect on the future. High taxation takes from businesses money that they could have invested in new equipment. Some of the government's spending reductions have the same negative effect on future productivity. Improvements are not made to roads, docks, and water supplies that would enable businesses to produce more efficiently, to transport their goods more economically. Clean-ups and repairs are not carried out. We leave to posterity a legacy of polluted lakes and rivers, of depleted forests, despite the fact that we have the capability of cleaning up those waters, of replanting those lands.

Because of unemployment Canada has failed to produce output that it has the physical capability of producing. We have lost that output, just as surely as if we had actually produced it and then dumped it into the sea. Those losses will never be made up. For human energy cannot be stored to be used at a later date. It's not like minerals in the ground, which, if not used now, are available for use in the future. Human energy that is not used is lost forever. We will never have the houses, factories, roads, and bridges that people who were unemployed in the past two decades could have built; we will never have the many and varied useful acts of service that could have been performed by people who were unemployed; we will never blot out the despondency and bitterness felt by people who hated to be idle. We will never undo the crimes and suicides that were committed by some people because they couldn't get jobs.

Waste, not savings, is the real consequence of much financial re-trenchment. A small but telling example occurred in 1979. As one element in the federal program of spending restraint, the Ministry of Fitness and Amateur Sport slashed its athletic travel grant to Maritime and western universities from $500,000 to $290,000. This grant had been introduced a year earlier to help university teams in these regions of Canada, who have to travel lengthy distances in order to play against one another. Thanks to the grant, teams were able to play more games away from home, sharpening their skills against appropriate competition. Reduction in the grant forced a reduction in the number and length of trips that teams could make. Players had less of the excitement and pleasure of trips to distant campuses; their athletic skills were not sharpened to the same degree. Fewer inter-university contests were glamourized by the participa-tion of visiting teams from far away.

These were not devastating losses for Canada. Small as it was, however, this deterioration was pointless because it achieved abso-lutely nothing. The $500,000 of grant money had been used to pay for travel on Air Canada flights. Those planes still flew; the usual crews were needed to operate them; they consumed exactly as much fuel as before. However, seats were now empty that might have been occupied by university athletes going to and from intercollegiate games. The government's financial saving did not produce a saving of labour and material. In real terms, the effect of the government's economy measure was not savings but waste – waste of the opportunity to provide people with something worthwhile at absolutely zero cost in labour and material.

As it turned out, the government did not even reap financial benefit. Since Air Canada belongs to the government, it was the government itself that took in $210,000 less in revenue after the cut. Taking this factor into account, Ottawa's financial gain from cutting the travel grant was zero.

The recession imposed by official policies of fiscal and monetary restraint in the early 1980s compelled private firms to react in ways that damaged the economy and burdened the country. A good many firms sharply reduced their spending to conform with the reduction in their revenues. They laid off employees, induced employees to take early retirement, held smaller inventories, kept equipment beyond normal replacement dates. The retrenchment measures were proudly designated by a set of buzzwords; firms "downsized," "trimmed the fat," became "lean and mean." Business journals published articles on how firms could "batten down the hatches to ride out the economic storm."

But in looking after themselves, firms did harm to others. The firm that "trimmed fat" by reducing staff put people out of work directly. The firm that bought less from suppliers obliged those suppliers to lay people off. Workers who lost their jobs were forced to cut their spending, causing reduction of sales and lay-offs in industries that produced and marketed consumer goods. People who were still working were frightened by the unemployment of others and cut their spending, too, further reducing the sales of consumer goods industries.

What was good for an individual firm was bad for the national economy. A firm might have become "lean and mean" by laying off somebody who was being paid $21,000 but producing only $20,000. But when that person became unemployed, the country lost $20,000 worth of output.

And the government lost money whenever a firm "downsized." People who were trimmed from payrolls no longer paid income tax and bought fewer goods on which sales tax was levied; the firms from which they bought less paid less business profit tax. Even worse, people who lost their jobs qualified for unemployment insurance. The government now had to give up to $12,000 to the worker who was laid off for producing $1,000 less than the firm was paying in salary.

Finance ministers and governors of the Bank of Canada, while emphasizing the vital importance of small firms to the Canadian economy, have applied policies that are particularly devastating to them.

Almost inevitably, small new firms are fragile, established typically by people with little or no business experience and with only slender financial resources. Unable to raise capital by selling securities, they depend entirely on bank credit for outside funds. They possess no reserves upon which to draw in an emergency; keeping alive is a daily struggle. Even a slight reversal – a small increase in operating costs, a small reduction in sales – can bring disaster.

While acknowledging the importance of small firms, public authorities have caused their casualty rate to be high. The Bank of Canada has allowed the interest rate to hit usurious levels, with devastating effect on small, weak firms that depend on bank borrowing. Finance ministers apply restrictive fiscal policies that put people out of work and reduce spending power in the country. While all businesses have difficulty as a consequence, the worst sufferers are small new firms. People who have less money to spend are less prepared to experiment with new products or new sources of supply; fewer people are generously inclined to give a new firm a chance, even if its product costs a little more. Because they have no accumulated reserves to tide them over, small new firms are less able to survive adversities.

Bankruptcies of businesses have soared to record levels in the 1980s, in considerable part because restrictive fiscal and monetary policies have brought contraction of demand for many products and, at the same time, steep increase in interest charges. Many farmers, dazzled by the sharp rise in agricultural prices of the 1970s, borrowed heavily to expand their operations. Bankers, equally dazzled, readily loaned them the money. In the 1980s the borrowers have been afflicted by the combination of flat or falling prices and hugely increased interest charges.

The burden of high interest rates is far from equally distributed.

There are particular victims: firms that have not accumulated their own capital and have had to borrow operating funds, farmers who have not inherited their farms and have had to borrow the money with which they acquired their land, livestock, and equipment. Record numbers of ordinary individuals were forced to declare personal bankruptcy in the 1980s recession, many because they had lost their jobs. Others were unable to meet the debt obligations they had undertaken, purely because of the huge increase in interest charges.

According to some analysts, the record number of bankruptcies in Canada in 1981 could not be blamed on federal economic policy. Detailed investigation of individual cases, they reported, revealed that the reasons for business failure were chiefly bad judgment and poor management – the same reasons for which enterprises failed in the very best of times. This claim is highly suspect. It declares in effect that a sudden, sharp deterioration occurred in the quality of business management in Canada. It implies that a large number of businesses that had been operating successfully for years suddenly lost their touch in 1981. It suggests that people who started up businesses in 1981 were far inferior to the people who had set up new businesses in the past and therefore had a higher failure rate.

On the contrary, the high probability is that the firms that went broke in 1981 were not managed any worse than before. Their managers no doubt made mistakes in 1981, but managers had made mistakes before, too. But previously, when economic conditions were better and interest rates were not oppressively high, a mistake did not bring on disaster. Its effects could be overcome; the operation could survive.

In the past a business might even have benefited from a mistake. Its manager would have learned what to do and what to avoid. The adverse experience would have useful consequences: the firm would carry on more effectively in the future. In a depressed economy, the same mistake would prove to be disastrous. A setback that in good times could be taken in stride now had lethal effect.

Since 1966, when the ceiling was removed, interest rates not only have been much higher but have fluctuated more widely. Before 1966 year-to-year changes in interest rates were slight; being as low as they were, there simply wasn't room for wide variations. The difference between the highest and lowest rate in any two-year period was less than 2 per cent. After 1966 the range of fluctuation was enormously wider; thus the mortgage interest rate rose from 11.80 per cent in August 1979 to 21.46 per cent in August 1981, fell to 13.26 per cent in April 1983, rose again to 14.96 per cent in August 1984, and fell to 11.75 per cent in November 1985.

This roller-coaster movement of interest rates has caused its own forms of harm, over and above those caused by the steep rise in their overall level. Any increase in the rate of interest brings a fall in the market value of bonds already issued; the greater the interest rate rise, the greater the fall in bond value. As a result of the wild rise in interest rates between 1979 and 1981, the value of bonds fell sharply; one typical issue, of bonds due to mature in 1999, fell by 37 per cent, from $88.94 to $55.62. Individuals and businesses that held considerable portfolios of government bonds suffered severe reductions in the total value of their assets; some were threatened with insolvency.

So long as interest rates changed very little over long periods, Canadian house-buyers were able to get twenty- and twenty-five-year mortgages on which the interest rate was fixed over the entire period of the mortgage. Lending institutions were badly burned, however, in the 1970s, when market interest rates rose sharply while they were still collecting the low interest stipulated in long-term mortgages that had been given out in the 1950s and 1960s. To ensure that they would not be caught that way again, mortgage companies refused to lend money at a fixed rate of interest for a period longer than five years; some refused to lend at a fixed rate for longer than three years; one-year and even six-month mortgages were introduced. In light of the risk that interest rates might rise sharply after they had given out a loan, lending institutions typically demanded a higher rate of interest on loans of longer duration; thus in December 1982, when the interest rate on a one-year mortgage was 12.50 per cent, the rate on a five-year mortgage was 14.34 per cent.

Borrowers who had to refinance their loans or mortgages in 1981 had to pay enormously increased interest charges. A person who had bought a house in 1976 with a $50,000 five-year mortgage found in 1981, when the mortgage had to be renewed, that the monthly interest charge would be $894 instead of $427.

The possibility of sharp movement in mortgage interest rates, either upward or downward, creates the possibility of heavy loss for anyone who takes out a mortgage for what proves to be the wrong duration. If the mortgage interest rate is going to rise, it would be best to take out a five-year mortgage; if the interest rate is going to be lower in the future, a one-year mortgage would be best. Ordinary individuals who want no part of this kind of uncertainty are forced to guess which way interest rates will go in the future. The one who guesses right might save thousands of dollars; the one who guesses wrong could be out of pocket thousands of dollars. The purchase of a house has become a gambling venture with a good deal in common with crap-shooting at Las Vegas, where the person who guesses right can win heavily and the person who guesses wrong can lose all.

Worse than the economic loss caused by unemployment is the psychological damage – the shock experienced by people who are laid off and compelled to lower their standard of living, the frustration and bitterness felt by people who spend their days in forced idleness. Heads of families suffer the shame of being unable to provide for their dependants. Studies in the U.S. and the U.K. indicate that higher rates of unemployment bring increases in crime, mental and physical illness, marital breakdown, and suicide. There is no reason to suppose that higher unemployment rates do not have the same effects in Canada.

Certainly the crime rate has increased. Canada's penitentiary population has soared to record levels in the 1980s. Our prisons have become crowded as never before, making it nearly impossible to carry out classification and sorting procedures, to operate programs of counselling and training that aim at rehabilitation. Harassed officials declare that they desperately need the additional prisons that have been projected, but whose construction has been deferred in accordance with the program of economic restraint. "Double-bunking" – placing two prisoners in a cell designed for one – has been resorted to, with explosive consequences in the form of prison riots.

Economic recession and penitentiary boom are not unrelated. A good many of the individuals who stage burglaries and hold-ups do so because they cannot get work. Persons who leave home in the hope of finding jobs elsewhere have those hopes dashed as regions that have been expanding stagnate instead; some, stranded and penniless, commit crimes to get the money they need to make their way back home.

The sharp economic downturn that occurred in 1981 was accompanied in Winnipeg by a near-doubling of the number of robberies. A local police inspector, drawing on ample experience, observed that when they can't get work, "people get pushed into situations they wouldn't normally find themselves in if they were employed. If we were in a situation where there was no unemployment and jobs were plentiful and money was plentiful, you'd see a decrease in these crimes."

The warden of Stony Mountain penitentiary noted to an interviewer, "It's been shown that the increase in the prison population is a direct result of the slumping economy." In light of the potentially explosive situation created in his institution by overcrowding, he added that he hoped we'd soon see some improvement in the economy.

Spending restraints contribute to crime in yet another way: reductions in security measures make crimes easier and safer to commit. Over the Easter weekend of 1979, thieves broke into an Ottawa post office and made off with $6 million of loot. They were able to pull off the job without being detected. As part of the federal government's restraint program, a planned alarm system had not been installed and the needed guards had not been hired.

The unemployment imposed by fiscal and monetary restraints has been a major factor in interracial conflicts in Canada. The especially high rate of unemployment in Quebec contributed to the rise and strength of the separatist movement: a good many unemployed and underemployed Quebeckers believed that under an independent regime they would be able to get jobs for which they were qualified. Concern about jobs was an important factor in the 1976 dispute about the use of French in Quebec air space. Anglophone air traffic controllers feared that they would lose their jobs if new regulations and procedures required personnel to be bilingual. The Manitoba government's undertaking in 1984 to make a number of civil service positions bilingual roused furious resentment among anglophones who feared a narrowing of job opportunities for themselves. A plenitude of alternative jobs would have eased the concerns of people who were disqualified from some positions by new government regulations. Because of the restraint program, that plenitude does not exist. Persons who lose their jobs because of bilingual requirements – or can't get jobs because of those requirements – face the prospect of unemployment.

The high interest rates imposed by the monetary authorities

sharply increase the advantage of inherited wealth and property, while sharply increasing the handicap of those whose parents have left them nothing. The people whose parents were poor, who have to borrow for major purchases, are obliged to hand over more money, which goes to the people whose parents left them handsome inheritances.

The increased significance of disparity in inheritance has been most dramatically demonstrated in agriculture. In the past, when interest rates had been 5 to 6 per cent, the handicap experienced by someone who had to buy a farm, instead of inheriting it, had not been oppressively large. Interest payments took a relatively small fraction of the farm's receipts. The double-digit interest rates of the 1970s and 1980s have required the person who buys a farm to make interest payments that are a very large fraction of receipts. In all too many cases these payments prove to be more than the farm can bear, bankruptcy being the consequence. The person who inherits a farm, on the other hand, and therefore is not saddled with monstrous interest charges, is able to operate comfortably under the same cost–price conditions.

A major justification of the wild increase in interest rates has been the need to keep up the foreign exchange rate of the Canadian dollar; more about this in Chapter 11. To save the Canadian population at large from having to pay marginally more for imports, sharply increased interest rates impose huge cost increases on specific groups of Canadians – those who have recently bought a house, tenants of new apartment blocks, small businesspeople, and farmers who have to borrow their operating capital. Crushing burdens are imposed on a victimized minority so that the rest of the population can buy imported goods and take trips abroad at no greater cost than before.

While the escalation of interest rates imposes varying degrees of harm on its victims, it confers sometimes large benefits on its favourites. Persons who have inherited wealth enjoy large increases in income; so do persons and firms that have accumulated savings on which they now receive hugely increased amounts of interest.

Increase in interest rates aggravates an already proceeding intergenerational transfer of wealth and income. The individuals who borrow money for such major purchases as a house or a car are typically younger persons who have not been able to save up the amount required. Those who provide the funds are typically older persons who have accumulated savings over many years. A rise in the rate of interest requires young borrowers to hand over more money to older lenders, for exactly the same financial service as before.

The advocates and practitioners of fiscal and monetary restraint take no account of the severe social problems that erupt from the unemployment that such a policy causes. And those social problems have economic costs: people who commit crimes damage the economy, make necessary large and costly police efforts, require enormous outlays on incarceration. The prisons in which they are confined require for their construction labour and materials that could be used to build factories, warehouses, schools, and hospitals. The personnel needed to staff the prisons could be working in enterprises that contribute to national output. They could be producing goods for sale in world markets; they could be producing goods and services that would reduce our dependence on imports.

People who become ill as a result of unemployment require treatment that is provided at public expense. People who lose their jobs are provided with publicly funded unemployment insurance or welfare. Since these costs are borne by other branches of government, they are ignored by those who frame and apply restrictive economic policies. It's altogether probable that if account were taken of these costs, it would be evident that, far from saving money by cutbacks that put people out of work, the government winds up spending more. Instead of the money being spent to achieve positive benefits, however, it is spent to remedy harm. The government is like the miser who begrudges spending money on nutritious food and, as a consequence, spends even more on the medicine he needs to counter the illness he has brought on himself by a poor diet.

SIX

Misguided Attacks

*Half a truth is often aired
and often proved correct.*
    PIET HEIN

For two decades now a paramount objective of federal government policy has been to bring inflation and unemployment down from their unacceptably high levels. The burden imposed by inflation has been exaggerated, however, while the harm done by unemployment has been understated. Believing inflation to be the greater menace and acting on a misguided diagnosis, Ottawa's authorities have applied policies that, while having mixed effects on the inflation problem, severely aggravated the unemployment problem.

Since the 1970s the "discomfort index" has been used as an indicator of national economic performance. The index is actually a very simple thing: the sum of the country's inflation rate and unemployment rate during any year. Canada's discomfort index was 20.1 in 1981, when the inflation rate was 12.5 per cent and the unemployment rate was 7.6 per cent; it rose to 22.2 in 1982 when the inflation rate was 11.2 and the unemployment rate 11.0; it fell to 15.1 in 1984 when the inflation rate was 4.1 and the unemployment rate 11.0.

In adding the inflation rate and the unemployment rate to produce a single aggregate figure, the index-makers implicitly assume that the two have equivalent effects, that a one-point increase in inflation causes exactly the same amount of harm as a one-point increase in unemployment. They assume that if an increase in one is matched by an equal decrease in the other, the public's level of well-being remains unchanged.

These assumptions are wildly at odds with reality; the two are far from being equivalent.

In 1933, the worst year of the Great Depression, the price level *fell* by 4.5 per cent and the unemployment rate was 22.3 per cent. The discomfort index was therefore 17.8, well below the figure of 20.1 for 1981, when the unemployment rate was 7.6 per cent and the inflation rate 12.5 per cent. According to this index, therefore, Canadians were worse off in 1981 than they had been in 1933 – a year when tens of thousands went hungry and lacked proper clothing and shelter, when tens of thousands of unemployed men rode freight trains, were put up in camps and fed in soup kitchens, when a good many children couldn't go to school because they didn't have shoes. An index that produces such a conclusion is an obscenity.

In Canada today every increase of one percentage point in the unemployment rate means that another 120,000 Canadians have lost their jobs. The country loses about $4 billion of output that those people would have produced had they been working. Several thousand of them will suffer severe stress, resulting in cases of mental and physical illness, crime, mental breakdown, family violence, suicide.

An increase of one percentage point in the inflation rate, on the other hand, could be accompanied by an increase in the number of people working in the country, as well as an increase in the production of goods. The overwhelming majority of Canadians get incomes that rise by at least the degree of inflation, so their purchasing power would not be reduced. They would just use slightly larger numbers in the consideration and management of their personal economies, because they would receive more income and pay more for what they buy. The relatively small number of Canadians whose incomes do not keep pace with inflation would indeed suffer a decline in their buying power if inflation rises, but that blow would be far less severe than the blow suffered by people who lose their jobs.

Canada's policy-makers, however, have taken the message of the discomfort index very seriously. Considering inflation and unemployment to be exactly equal evils, they have been quite prepared to apply programs that imposed unemployment in order to prevent inflation. A one-percentage-point increase in unemployment is considered justified if it brings about a one-percentage-point reduction in inflation. This has been a calculus offensive to common sense as well as morality.

According to after-dinner speakers, inflation is a curse that afflicts absolutely everybody. Everyone, they declare, is victimized by rising prices; everyone is made worse off; no one benefits. This constantly repeated assertion is blatantly false. Money paid out by buyers doesn't disappear into thin air; it's received by sellers. If buyers are paying higher prices for what they buy, sellers must be receiving higher prices for what they sell. What buyers denounce as inflation is what sellers approve as welcome and appropriate increases in their receipts.

Borrowers also benefit from inflation. They have obligated themselves to pay designated sums as interest each year and, on a specified future date, to repay the amount of their loans. Every rise in the price level reduces the real value of the payments they must make, reduces the amount of purchasing power they give up in making those payments.

The inflation that has occurred in Canada in the past twenty years has not caused a decline in the material well-being of the Canadian people. A country's consumption is basically determined by its production; if it produces more, its people can have more, despite whatever inflation occurs. Canada's experience bears this out. No decline occurred in the material well-being of the Canadian people over the years from 1972 to 1982, when the inflation rate averaged 9.7 per cent, a much higher figure than in any ten-year period in the country's peacetime history. Nevertheless, Canadians were better off in material terms in 1982 than they had been in 1972. While the consumer price index rose by 151 per cent over that ten-year period, the weekly earnings of industrial workers rose by an average of 160 per cent, so that they were slightly better off in 1982 than they had been in 1972, despite inflation that had averaged nearly 10 per cent.

What is true for the average person, of course, is not true for everybody. There certainly are people who have become worse off because of inflation. These are people whose money incomes have not increased at all or have increased by less than the rate of inflation. But what has been lost by these people has been gained by others. Many people have had increases in income that were above the inflation rate. Their increases in buying power have been gained, in part, from other people's decreases.

The people who have been hardest hit in the past twenty years have been the ones who lost their jobs or couldn't get jobs. A person who lost a job suffered a far greater decline in buying power than did a person whose income was eroded by inflation. As well, the unemployed worker suffered a severe psychological blow. Jobless people who used up their unemployment insurance credits and had to go on welfare suffered the humiliation of dependence on charity.

Ironically, it is not inflation that puts people out of work. The shortage of jobs is caused not by inflation but by the remedy applied to end inflation. It has been the restraints applied to public and private-sector spending, the curbs on credit, and high rates of interest that have limited the total of job opportunity in Canada. The amount of harm suffered by people who cannot get jobs and the production lost to the country because they aren't working have far exceeded the harm suffered in Canada in the form of actual decline in real income because of inflation. The remedy applied against inflation in the past twenty years has done more harm than the inflation problem itself.

The inflation that Canada experienced after the mid-1960s was unquestionably harmful: it brought about unfair redistribution of income; it caused worry and created a climate of uncertainty, which damaged the country's economic performance. But probably the worst effect was to move the government to apply the anti-inflation policy that it chose – policy that condemned the country to large-scale unemployment.

"Natural rate of unemployment" is a term widely used by economists. It represents the assumption that a substantial degree of unemployment is unavoidable in any country and harm would result from attempts to bring the unemployment rate down to a lower figure. Any such attempt would prove to be a failure and would merely aggravate the country's inflation problem.

The basis of the concept is that so long as there is a sufficiently high rate of unemployment in the country, the ranks of the unemployed are likely to include people with every type of ability and skill. Any business that needs staff is able to recruit whatever type of person it needs from the ranks of the unemployed. It pays them only at the going rates; they are happy to get the jobs.

As the number of the unemployed declines, however, their ranks no longer include people with every type of ability and skill. Now a firm that needs additional workers of a particular type can get them only by luring them away from their present employers, by offering them higher rates of pay than they are getting. Firms that are threatened with loss of key staff match the offers made by outsiders. The upshot is that production costs become higher for everybody when the amount of unemployment in the country decreases.

While superficially plausible, this thesis is seriously misleading. It grossly exaggerates what has been a minor factor in Canada's inflationary experience and totally ignores a factor of preponderant importance.

Relative to the total size of the national labour force, the number of workers for whom employers bid competitively has been minute. At no time during the past two decades have such workers constituted as much as 1 per cent of Canada's labour force. For the other 99 per cent, wage rates have been set through negotiation between employers and union representatives, by minimum wage laws, by employers who simply paid the going rate.

Since the pay of only a tiny number of workers has been increased by the competitive bidding of employers, the significance to the economy of their increases has been minimal. Even if employers wound up paying double the going rate to scarce workers, the effect would be to raise the country's total wage bill by less than 1 per cent.

What is really significant when employers bid up the pay of 1 per cent of the country's workers is the reaction of the other 99 per cent. If the big pay gains achieved by a few workers impel the 99 per cent to insist on increases, then the effect on the economy becomes substantial. While a 10-per-cent increase in the pay of 1 per cent of the country's workers will have negligible effect on the country's inflation rate, a 10-per-cent increase achieved by 99 per cent of the workers will have a substantial effect. The unspoken assumption of the "natural rate of unemployment" concept is that when the unemployment rate falls and the pay of some types of workers is bid up, other workers insist on corresponding increases in their pay. That is what causes the inflation, not the reduction in unemployment.

By the same token, many people make the assumption, as a matter of course, that an increase in the unemployment rate is bound to be deflationary. Exactly the opposite is true: an increase in unemployment is, in itself, *inflationary*. For workers who lose their jobs do not, in our day and age, lose all their spending power. They continue to spend money, drawn from savings or given to them as unemployment insurance or welfare assistance. The country's price level edges up, as a consequence of the change in balance between the supply of goods in the country and the demand. Supply drops considerably because those workers are no longer contributing to production; demand drops only slightly because they continue to have purchasing power, nearly as much as before.

Unemployment is in fact deflationary only if it intimidates workers into reducing their wage demands. If it does that, then it reduces the size of an increase in production cost and thereby holds down the size of price increases. If unemployment fails to exercise this effect – if the unemployment of others does not induce workers to moderate their pay demands – then its effect is purely inflationary.

An increase in spending that puts unemployed people to productive work can in fact be *deflationary*. Suppose that a person drawing unemployment insurance of $160 a week gets a job at $300 a week. If he contributes over $140 a week to the country's production the price level will fall. For an additional $140 of spending, the country will get more than an additional $140 of goods; the average of all prices will be lowered.

If inflation occurs, for whatever reason, then obviously workers are entitled to "catch-up" increases in pay to recover a level of real income that has been reduced by inflation, and they are entitled to further increases in pay that will enable them to "keep up" with inflation expected to occur in the future.

Both catch-up and keep-up increases in rates of pay have, however, contributed to the inflation problem. Catch-up increases received by everyone have failed to restore previous levels of real income. The reason is simple. If only one small group of people receives a pay increase of, say, 20 per cent, then the price level is unaffected; the small group's purchasing power would rise by 20 per cent. But if absolutely everybody gets a pay increase of 20 per cent, then production costs and prices will increase by that amount. Though all got increases of 20 per cent, no one is better off than before. If everybody catches up, then nobody catches up.

"Keep-up" increases in pay, whether in the form of raises in wage rates or cost-of-living allowances geared to the inflation rate, also raise production costs, requiring an increase in prices. Protection against inflation causes the inflation against which the protection needs to be provided.

Canada's recent experience exemplifies this. Between 1975 and 1982 the average increase in weekly earnings in Canada was 10 per cent; during that period the inflation rate averaged 9.6 per cent. Between 1982 and 1984, when the average increase in earnings dropped to 6.5 per cent, the inflation rate dropped to 5 per cent. The inflation rate dropped when pay increases fell below the figures needed to "keep up with inflation."

On May 29, 1979, Gerald Bouey, the governor of the Bank of Canada, appeared before the Senate Standing Committee on National Finance to explain and defend the Bank's monetary policies. No doubt he did not realize it, but the explanation he provided damningly criticized those policies. In his testimony Bouey underlined the limitations of monetary policy, declaring:

> I want to emphasize that monetary policy is a financial instrument and it operates directly on financial flows in the economy. . . . The way in which the real economic variables in the economy respond to changes in financial flows is heavily dependent on other policies and practices throughout the economy about which the central bank can do very little.

He then went on to state the prerequisites for successful application of a restrictive monetary policy: "The point here is that the success of monetary policy in lowering the rate of inflation requires the adjustment of price and cost behaviour to the lower rate of monetary expansion."

Those statements begged crucial questions. What if the preconditions of success didn't exist? What if, throughout the economy, policies and practices were followed that prevented the "real variables" – prices, wages, production, and costs – from responding appropriately to the central bank's regulation of monetary flows? What if prices and costs did not adjust to the Bank's lower rate of monetary expansion?

This is in fact what happened throughout the 1970s. Between 1973 and 1979 Arab countries increased the price of oil approximately tenfold, and the price of food soared as a consequence of the poor Soviet harvest of 1972. Within Canada strong trade unions, in both the private and public sectors, effectively insisted on wage increases far above the Bank's target rates of monetary expansion; giant corporations used their market power to raise their profit margins even more. Evidently the Arabs, the U.S.S.R.'s weather, Canadian labour, and Canadian business weren't aware of the Bank of Canada's target monetary growth rates or, at least, didn't pay much attention.

A course of action is not warranted if the indispensable pre-conditions to its success do not exist; on its own terms it must fail. Even worse, it may cause positive harm. Given adverse conditions, that action may aggravate the problem it is intended to alleviate. However brilliantly it would have succeeded had the appropriate conditions existed, it may have disastrous consequences if followed when those conditions did not exist. Thus in wartime an infantry unit might, with artillery support, launch a successful assault on a vital enemy position. Without the artillery support the attack would lead only to a futile massacre.

The economic equivalent of a failed infantry assault in fact occurred in Canada from 1975 to 1981, when the Bank of Canada was progressively reducing the growth rate of the Canadian money supply. Prices and costs did not decline in the manner upon which – according to the governor of the Bank – the success of that strategy depended. It certainly did not achieve its object of reducing inflation; as a matter of fact, the average inflation rate of 9.6 per cent experienced over that seven-year period was far above the inflation rate in any other seven-year period in Canada's peacetime history. The inflation rate declined only after the policy of progressively reducing the money supply by targeted amounts was abandoned. Monetary growth rates that were kept below the rise in the price level acted like a brake pressing down on the economy, causing an unemployment rate that averaged 7.8 per cent, a rate well in excess of that experienced in any seven-year period since the Great Depression of the 1930s. The country was denied the benefit of having goods and services that it was physically capable of producing but whose production was prevented by high interest rates; it lost investment in physical plant that would have made a larger output possible in the future.

In 1982 Bouey acknowledged that it was impossible to tell just what constituted the country's money supply. Apparently from 1975 to 1981 the Bank had been reducing each year, in carefully measured degree, something whose nature was uncertain and whose dimensions were unknown. The assessment Bouey gave in 1979 of the possibilities and limitations of monetary policy as anti-inflation strategy was absolutely correct. Unfortunately, in his administration of the Bank he ignored the logic of his own analysis. By his own description he was like a military commander who orders an infantry attack on a confusingly described objective, hoping that the vital artillery cover will somehow materialize.

SEVEN

Government Under Siege

The people's government made for the people, made by the people, and answerable to the people.
DANIEL WEBSTER

In Canada, as in other countries, the national government now plays a much larger economic role than it did in the past. In addition to providing the traditional services of protection, education, and the like, it operates individual enterprises, closely regulates private-sector economic activity, redistributes income, and attempts to keep the national economy on an even keel.

During the 1980s "big government" has come under heavy attack, especially in the United States and Great Britain. Critics charge that the government is attempting to do more than it can afford, more than it can effectively manage; however well intentioned, many of its activities do more harm than good. Defenders of "big government," on the other hand, insist that in a modern industrialized society the political authorities must play a larger role than they did in former times, when the country was predominantly agricultural and life far simpler; what's more, a national government's financial capacity is not nearly so limited as critics claim.

Government, according to the strident proclamations of some prominent politicians and businesspeople, is absolutely unproductive. Moreover, the taxation by which it is supported hampers and burdens private enterprise. Since it is only private enterprise that actually produces goods and services, they declare, it's essential to minimize the weight of a heavy and useless burden.

The private sector, on the other hand, is colourfully likened to a coiled spring that is compressed by heavy weights – a meddlesome bureaucracy, and heavy taxation imposed to furnish the salaries of the meddling bureaucrats and to provide overly generous allowances to the old, the poor, the sick, and the unemployed. Removal of these weights would release the coiled spring. If private enterprise were relieved of its burdens, it would expand dynamically and soon generate all the jobs needed for full employment.

Moreover, those jobs would be genuinely productive. Employees would be producing goods and services that are useful and saleable, instead of loafing around government offices where their work – when they do any – consists of putting obstacles in the way of people who are really producing something.

This sweeping condemnation of public-sector activity combined with exaltation of the private sector is wildly unbalanced. From it the conclusion follows that a public library represents a wasteful expenditure of citizens' money while a tavern that features female mud-wrestling is a valuable community asset. A lifeguard at a public beach is of no use to anybody; a sidewalk barker who draws passersby into a sleazy night club contributes solidly to national productivity.

Differences in viewpoint understandably exist in respect to the desirability of some public regulatory bodies. They cost a great deal to maintain and their rulings have negative as well as positive consequences. Different people will, quite legitimately, come to different conclusions as to where their cost–benefit balance lies.

Some people feel that too many free-loaders are taking advantage of public welfare programs and that the assistance given to the needy is too generous. Others believe that abuse of these programs is slight and that yet more aid should be given to those in need. Such differences of view are inevitable and will likely always exist. The great bulk of government services are clearly essential to the community, however, and are in fact indispensable to the operation of the private sector. Private businesses depend on government-maintained police and fire departments for protection against theft and destruction. Their trucks carrying materials to plants and merchandise to customers roll over government-maintained roads, streets, and bridges. Government-supported schools furnish young people with the education they will need in order to be effective employees of private enterprise establishments.

If these functions were not provided by government, they would have to be provided by private enterprise. And they would still have to be paid for. The only difference would be that instead of being paid for by taxation, they would be paid for by fees charged to users.

It's quite possible that services now provided by government would be more efficiently provided by private enterprise. Anyone who has ever worked for government is painfully aware that its departments are often overstaffed, that its employees frequently show inadequate concern to achieve careful, waste-free operation. However, it simply isn't feasible for private enterprise to offer many of the services provided by government. It would be out of the question, for instance, for private enterprise to maintain police and fire departments, to provide street lighting, to operate free schools.

If essential services are inefficiently provided, the best remedy is not to provide fewer of them but to eliminate the inefficiency. If less money is spent on an inefficiently provided public service, the effect may simply be that the community gets less of something it vitally needs – and suffers accordingly.

The scorn heaped on the public sector keeps us from acquiring large numbers of highly desirable jobs. We are repeatedly warned that public-sector spending to generate jobs would only "throw money" at the unemployment problem, that it would at best create a few jobs that were temporary and pointless. But we badly need extension and improvement of public works and public services; money spent for these purposes would generate jobs that were permanent and productive.

An enormous number of public works could be carried out in Canada that would make the national economy more efficient and productive and the lives of individual Canadians safer and more agreeable. Improvement of highways and street pavements, con-struction of more bridges across rivers, and modernization of docks would reduce transportation costs for businesses and private indi-viduals. Every year people are killed at level rail crossings; lives would be saved if those crossings were replaced by underpasses. Storms blow down telephone and power lines, knocking out service to thousands of people; that disruption would be ended if the lines were buried underground. Lakes and rivers are rendered unfit for swimming by sewage dumped into them; a swim in Lake Ontario has been a potentially lethal exercise for years, and 3 million To-rontonians have been denied a pleasure they might have had. The construction of a modern sewage gathering and disposal system would enable them to enjoy fully the magnificent body of water on their doorstep.

The physical capability of carrying out these projects exists in Canada and has existed here for a long time. The hundreds of thousands of construction workers, engineers, and technicians who have been unemployed during the past dozen years could have built such projects in the time that they were unemployed. Not only these people would have had jobs had these projects been undertaken; construction workers would have spent their earnings on food, clothing, housing, entertainment, and so on, generating jobs in these industries as well. The country's unemployment problem could have been far smaller than it actually was.

In a "fireside chat" Prime Minister Trudeau once cautioned the people of Canada not to expect very much during the current difficult times. A large number of Canadians were unemployed and therefore had less spending power. The government, too, he declared, was in straitened circumstances and unable to undertake projects that were unquestionably desirable. It could not build additional public works and provide additional public services, even though these would be beneficial to the country and would generate jobs for unemployed people. The nation simply could not afford such "make-work" projects at this time. We could expect to have more public works and public services only when prosperity returned and we could then afford them.

Trudeau's homily was reminiscent of the attitude of John, a Regina mechanic who was laid off for about six months in 1981. His wife suggested that while he was out of a job he could spend his time fixing up the house. A leaky roof needed repair; the front steps were actually dangerous; putty on the storm windows would keep drafts out in winter and reduce heating bills; the kitchen and living room would be much brighter and more cheerful if they were given a coat of paint. Instead of just lounging around the house, despondent and frustrated at his idleness, John could be doing all these jobs, which would make the house safer, more agreeable to live in, cheaper to maintain. Its market value would increase; the gain that John achieved in the form of savings on heating bills and increase in value of the house might be about as great as the money he would have earned had he been working at his job.

John, however, snarled at her not to bother him with her "make-work" projects. His months of unemployment were not the time to make these repairs and improvements to the house; the proper time would be when he was once again working full-time at his job.

Canada is our national house. If Canadians can't have a regular job, then, rather than just be idle, they could be repairing and improving their house. They would save themselves from the frustration and bitterness of having nothing to do; the work they did would enable them to live more economically, more pleasantly; it would have a cash value nearly equivalent to the money they would have earned had they been working at their jobs.

Trudeau's logic corresponded to John's. He considered the years of Canadians' unemployment the wrong time for them to repair and improve their national house. They should do that only when they were fully employed at their regular jobs.

What's needed is the simple common sense that is applied as a matter of course in a business. In any well-run enterprise, workers never stand about idly, drawing pay for doing nothing. Whenever demand for its product slackens, management will energetically attempt to increase sales by advertising, by special promotions, by price reductions. If the usual production processes do not require the services of everyone on the payroll, the management will assign special tasks; it will have workers do clean-ups and repairs, carry out improvements; it may arrange training programs that will increase workers' competence so that they will do their regular work more effectively in the future. Whatever benefit accrues to the firm from these measures is achieved at zero cost, since the workers had to be paid anyway and would otherwise have done nothing.

The same kind of intelligent management can be applied in the administration of a national economy. Whenever workers would otherwise be idle, the authorities can arrange that they be usefully occupied, either in the public sector by government spending or in the private sector by tax reduction, subsidization, and reduction of interest rates. After all, workers for whom there is no work do not disappear; they remain in the country – on the national payroll, in effect – and are supported by the rest of the community. They may as well do something useful; whatever they contribute by their efforts is net gain for the community, for otherwise they would have contributed nothing.

In an authoritarian society the waste of unemployment is prevented by fiat: the ruler simply orders people to do tasks when otherwise they would be idle. In our democratic society, where work is done not on the command of a dictator but in response to the offer of pay, the authorities can prevent unemployment by arranging that people be offered pay to do work.

A good many people oppose proposals along these lines, insisting that the government is incapable of generating jobs and that its attempts to do so would have disastrous financial consequences. No small irony is involved here. The most vehement opponents of government action to prevent the waste of unemployment are among the most stalwart exponents of the free enterprise system. These are the people who insist, in effect, that a free enterprise system can't operate like a well-managed business and that democracy is less able than dictatorship to apply good business sense.

The irony is compounded by another fact. It is the business community that most vociferously opposes increases in government spending–when those increases would mean more government purchases from businesses and larger incomes for their customers. Private-sector representatives demand cuts in government spending–cuts that will mean smaller government purchases from businesses and unemployment for their customers. What they demand, vehemently and repeatedly, is amputation of a hand that feeds them.

Canada's population being one-tenth that of the U.S., many people assume, as a matter of course, that the appropriate figure for any Canadian activity is one-tenth that of its U.S. counterpart. If our figure is greater, it is excessive; if it is less, it is deficient.

Using this measurement, it appears that we have too much government; our governments do too much, spend too much, incur excessively large deficits. But before we accept this judgment, we should have the answers to two highly relevant questions. Does the U.S. economy at all times perform so well that it is always an example worthy of being followed? Second, are Canada's circumstances the same, so that policies that work well in the U.S. can be expected to serve us equally well?

The answer to both questions is an emphatic no. The U.S. economy has at times performed very badly: during the 1970s its rates of inflation and unemployment were even worse than ours and many Americans suffered declines in their standard of living.

But even if the U.S. economy were performing well, there would still be compelling reasons for applying different economic policies. The fact that the U.S. population is ten times ours means that between us there must be not just differences in degree but vital differences in kind. In an industry where the U.S. market can support ten firms of the most efficient size, the Canadian market can support only one. In such an industry the U.S. relies on having the competition that is assured by the existence of ten rival firms; in Canada we can have only one firm – a monopoly. Some kind of government intervention will be needed in Canada – where none is needed in the U.S. – to assure that the monopoly firm does not abuse its power by charging exorbitant prices or providing inferior service.

The size of the U.S. private sector ensures that it will be able to furnish capital on a gigantic scale, enough to finance the very largest of industrial projects. In Canada huge industrial projects are beyond the capacity of our private sector: they can be carried out only if government provides financial assistance. It is no coincidence that U.S. railways were financed entirely by private capital, but Canada's railway system was built with huge government grants and loans. Without that financial support from government, the lines could not have been built. In fact, government has played a major economic role here from the earliest days, when settlers depended on military garrisons for markets as well as for protection.

The majority of manufacturing and resource exploitation is done in Canada by branch plants whose head office is in another country – the U.S., in most cases. Throughout the world very little research and development is done in branch plants: these are generally headquarters functions, carried out at the parent plant. The consequence is that Canada's private sector does very little research and product development. Graduates of our universities and colleges who become qualified for such work have to move to the U.S., where the work is being done. If Canada is to be in the forefront of the world's technology, developing new techniques and new products – and providing appropriate employment in Canada for highly qualified Canadians – then government must play a far larger role in the financing of research here than it does in the U.S.

Canada's sheer geographic extent means that transportation is one of the major costs of operating the national economy. Everywhere and inevitably transportation is a government responsibility: governments must build and maintain roads, build and operate air fields, and so on. Here, too, government in Canada necessarily plays a relatively larger role than government in the U.S.

The fact is that in any modern industrialized country, government must play a large and critically important role. It must arrange for national defence, for the protection of persons and property, for the administration of justice. It must build and maintain the national transportation system and the national education system; it must give aid to the helpless; it must provide necessary services that private enterprise cannot provide. It must intervene in the economy to stabilize its working and to ensure that paramount public needs are being served. The role is a vital one; as a matter of course, it should be filled sufficiently and well.

We need more effort, not less, applied in these areas. The jobs that can be generated here through the additional application of government funds would be more productive than a good many jobs in the private sector and would contribute more to the country's productivity and more to the public's well-being.

The word "cost" in everyday speech denotes the amount of money that has to be given up to get something. The phrase "real cost" denotes the actual services or goods that must be given up by a purchaser. Thus the real cost to a worker of a pair of shoes is the hours of work put in to earn them; from another perspective, the cost of these shoes is the shirts that could have been bought instead of the shoes. The real cost to Canada of building new school buildings is the housing that could have been built by the construction labour and materials that went into the schools.

If a country's productive power is fully employed, the monetary cost of anything – the cost in dollars – corresponds to its real cost. If at a time of full employment Canada launches a $1-billion school construction program, the labour and materials required would have to be taken away from other forms of production – probably housing construction. The real cost of the schools would then be the $1 billion worth of housing that could have been built if the school construction program had not been undertaken.

If, however, there is productive power in the country that is not being used, the situation is very different. If there are unemployed workers in the construction trades and in construction material industries, then a school-building program could be carried out by people who would otherwise have been idle. There need be no reduction in the number of houses built; the real cost of the school construction program would be zero.

It could even turn out that the monetary cost of the program would be zero as well. Because of the employment it provided, the government would pay out less in unemployment insurance and welfare while its tax collections would rise. Workers who got jobs would pay more income tax; when they spent their new earnings, the government would collect more sales tax, and more profit tax from the firms they patronized. Instead of being burdens on the federal treasury, a great many people would now be contributors to it. A recent study estimated that for every $1 million the government spends on public works projects it gets back, in tax revenues and unemployment insurance saving, about $400,000. The net cost to the government is therefore only about 60 per cent of its actual expenditures.

The net cost could turn out to be much smaller still. If the improvement in employment and sales prompted businesses to expand, then the government would collect additional tax revenue and save more UI money as a result of the jobs created by this private-sector expansion. If Ottawa's spending of $1 billion on schools caused private businesses to spend $1.5 billion on construction of new plant, the additional tax revenue and UI savings would total $1 billion; the net cost to Ottawa of its $1-billion outlay would be zero. And if the private sector were induced to spend more than $1.5 billion on construction, Ottawa would get back more than its $1 billion; the program would bring about not an increase but a reduction in the federal deficit.

Even if these highly desirable consequences didn't occur, a program of spending on public works could still be worth undertaking. The jobs gained, together with the results of the work, could be well worth the government's outlay.

There are today in Canada thousands of unemployed scientists, engineers, and technicians who could be doing research on pollution, energy, and computer technology. The real cost of having them do the research of which they are capable would be zero. There are thousands of unemployed construction tradespeople who could be building houses, stores, factories, roads. The real cost to Canada of all that construction would be zero.

That research will be done, those houses, stores, factories, and roads will be built, only if the government puts up the necessary money, either by spending it itself or by reducing taxes, thereby enabling and inducing the private sector to spend it.

Proposals that the government generate productive jobs for unemployed workers are opposed on account of their "cost." There is no recognition that the real cost to Canada of anything produced by someone who would otherwise have been unemployed is zero. And there is very little recognition that the net monetary cost to the government is bound to be far less than its actual outlays, and that, in any case, what is "cost" to the government is income for individual Canadians.

A telling example of this financial myopia occurred in April 1983 at the time that Marc Lalonde delivered his budget. The day before he was to read his budget speech, a leak occurred of how much the government proposed to spend on job-generating public works that year and how big it expected the deficit to be. To preserve the tradition that what the minister of finance reads out in his budget speech is not revealed beforehand, the government altered the figures overnight: Lalonde announced an amount for job generation in 1983 that was larger than originally budgeted by $100 million and predicted that the deficit would accordingly be greater by $100 million.

That alteration of the books revealed the Ottawa mind set. It took no account of the elementary consideration that if unemployed people get jobs, Ottawa no longer has to pay them unemployment insurance. It made no allowance for the equally elementary fact that if people get jobs and therefore have higher incomes, they pay more income tax and spend more money on goods on which sales tax is collected; and their additional spending increases the earnings of businesses, who consequently pay more profit tax. As indicated above, the financial benefits that accrue to Ottawa when the average unemployed Canadian gets a job have been estimated at 40 per cent of his wage. If, therefore, Ottawa increased its spending on job generation by $100 million in 1983, its deficit would rise not by $100 million but at most by $60 million.

In making its financial calculations, the Department of Finance evidently assumes that unemployed workers who get jobs continue to collect unemployment insurance, that despite having higher incomes they pay the same income tax, that although they have more money in their pockets they spend no more. With this kind of bookkeeping by the people responsible for the Canadian economy, it's no wonder that we have double-digit unemployment and the prospect that it will continue for years.

Politicians and economic commentators repeatedly emphasize that

Ottawa just doesn't have the money to fund additional programs – or even to maintain already existing programs at their present level. They make the point with homely, colourful language: "The cupboard is bare." "The government is broke." "Canada is bankrupt." The implication is that the federal treasury is a box containing coins, and there are now very few coins left.

This is a primitive and wholly misleading view of federal finance; the federal government's money is not a heap of coins. Neither is anyone else's, for that matter; what is reverently referred to as "hard cash" consists today of slips of coloured paper and notations in bankers' deposit books, or electronic impressions in their computers. The amount of money possessed by anyone depends on numbers printed on pieces of paper or recorded in computer memories.

The federal government can at any time obtain additional funds by using its power of taxation – its authority to simply order people to hand money over. It must of course use that power with discretion. Politicians who impose excessive taxation are likely to be voted out of office. On the other hand, the public wants public services and recognizes that they must be paid for by taxation; an administration that taxed too little and provided too few public services could also be turned out of office. So the federal government's income is not a specific, unchangeable amount; it is determined by the political judgment of the government itself.

Like a business and other levels of government, the federal government can get money by borrowing. It can borrow from individuals and financial institutions, as do all other borrowers, and, in addition, from a source to which it alone has access. It, and it alone, can borrow from our central bank, the Bank of Canada.

The federal government owns and controls the Bank of Canada. It borrows by selling the Bank its bonds, receiving in payment currency that the Bank prints or a deposit that it writes in its books. The Bank cannot refuse to buy, and there is no physical or statutory limit to the amount of bonds the government can sell to the Bank, or the amount of money the Bank can create to pay for those bonds.

But while there is no legal limit to the amount of money the federal government can obtain by selling bonds to the Bank of Canada – or other lenders – there is a limit imposed by judgment. The bigger the government's debt, the more interest it will have to pay; the more it borrows and spends, the greater will be the possibility of inflation in the country.

The issue of how much the government should borrow, in the country's capital markets and from the Bank of Canada, is a matter of judgment on which totally divergent views are held. On the one hand there is the belief, widely held in the business community, that the federal government's debt is already excessively large, imposing a monstrous burden of interest charges on the country, and that large additional borrowing would severely aggravate the problem. On the other hand there is the view, held by many economists, that so long as the government borrows within Canada, its debt is not a burden on the country because all the interest payments will be made to Canadians.

Here is the critical issue: additional borrowing by the federal government, with the money spent on useful public works, would generate jobs for unemployed people and bring a physical improvement of the country. At what point, however, would that borrowing become excessive, in that the benefits of increased employment and physical improvement would be more than offset by the addition to the government's burden of interest payments and aggravation of the country's inflation problem? The evidence from the past bearing on this issue is complex and contradictory; intelligent and well-informed people can hold diametrically opposing views. The assertion, however, that the government "just hasn't got the money" is a crude and ignorant interjection into the debate.

The claim that the federal government "just hasn't got the money" is made in peacetime only. In wartime the government has readily obtained all the money it needed to pay for an all-out war effort.

A host of experts insist that in fiscal matters the government is no different from a private firm and must abide by the same limitations. It must limit its spending to its income; if it borrows, it must borrow only as much as it will be able to repay out of future income. This is perfectly true for other levels of government – but not for the national government of a country. For such a government has two transcending powers that totally differentiate its fiscal capability from that of a private firm. First, whereas a firm depends for its income upon the public's willingness to buy its products, the government has unlimited power of taxation – the authority to order citizens to hand over money, in whatever amount it designates. Secondly, it has the authority to simply create the kind of money that circulates

within the country. In light of these powers that a national government possesses, there is absolutely no comparison between its fiscal
capability and that of a private firm within the country. The correct
private-sector analogy to a national government is not a business
but a hold-up artist who resorts to counterfeiting whenever his
victims don't provide him with all the income he requires.

According to some experts (and non-experts), Canada's program of
unemployment insurance is responsible for a large part of its unemployment problem. Many people know of individuals who have
deliberately quit their jobs in order to live off unemployment insurance; many know of persons drawing UI benefits who are very
slow to get another job. Articles in learned journals give statistical
analyses showing that Canada's unemployment insurance scheme is
causing the unemployment rate to be about 2 per cent higher than
it would otherwise be.

The proposition that unemployment insurance increases the
number of unemployed begs some questions, however. If somebody
quits a job, that job becomes available for someone else. And if
someone else takes it, no change occurs in the number of the country's unemployed. A change occurs only in the identities of the
unemployed and of the employed. Instead of Smith being jobless
and Jones working, Jones is jobless and Smith is working. Between
the two of them there is still only one job, and their unemployment
rate continues to be 50 per cent.

If a person quits a job, the amount of unemployment in the
country will increase only if there is no one else willing and able to
take it. There would be one more unemployed person, and one more
unfilled job. Unemployment insurance could properly be blamed for
an increase in unemployment only if it gives rise to an increase in
the number of unfilled jobs. But literally hundreds of people apply
whenever a decent job is advertised, and it is snapped up at once.

A strong case can be made for the proposition that unemployment insurance serves to *reduce* the country's unemployment rate.
For people who lose their jobs thereby lose the spending power
conferred on them by their pay. That spending power enabled them
to make purchases that generated jobs for other people, who produced
goods they needed and wanted.

UI benefits partially maintain unemployed people's spending
power and therefore enable them to keep on providing work for

other people. The closer the benefits are to the income they used to earn, the smaller will be the decline in their spending power and the smaller will be the reduction in the amount of work they generate for other people.

Economic textbooks recognize this function performed by unemployment insurance and label it an "automatic stabilizer." It serves as a stabilizer because it counteracts a decline in the economy that puts people out of work, limiting the spread of the contagion of unemployment. It is "automatic" because it requires no judgment or decision-making; workers who lose their jobs routinely qualify for unemployment insurance benefits.

The need for such a stabilizer was powerfully demonstrated during the Great Depression of the 1930s, when there was no such thing as unemployment insurance. People who lost their jobs lost their spending power and therefore transmitted their unemployment to others. With no brake to slow its momentum, the economy kept spiralling downward, and the unemployment rate reached the 20- to 25-per-cent range. The unemployment insurance program that we have today was instituted as a result of that experience, to help individuals and to serve the economy by moderating the repercussions of any initial decline. It continues to perform both functions.

EIGHT

The Leash on Production

If little labour, little are our gaines,
Man's fortunes are according to his paines.
HERRICK

The object of any economy is to produce useful goods, as many as possible with the means available. The economic policies followed by the federal government in the past two decades have had the effect of keeping idle a large part of Canada's productive capacity, so that our output of goods has been much smaller than we were physically capable of producing. The government refused to apply policies that would have put unemployed people to work and increased national output, because of the financial costs they entailed. In its calculations, however, it did not take into account all of the financial benefits that would follow from an increase in production and a reduction in unemployment. Our free enterprise system is not so perverse as to render financially unacceptable economic activities that are both physically possible and desirable. Whenever this kind of contradiction appears, it is because of errors or omissions in calculation, not because it genuinely exists.

"In these difficult times we must exercise restraint." This caution has been given by innumerable politicians and economic experts. But restraint can be in a variety of forms; not all of them are useful. We should indeed restrain our spending on imports when there are Canadian products that are just as good; we should limit our borrowing in other countries; we should restrain increases in our pay that are in excess of productivity gains. These forms of restraint are helpful: they will help keep Canadians employed; they will keep us from piling up big debts to foreigners; they will prevent inflation in Canada.

There are other forms of restraint that are harmful, however.

Restraints on spending that put Canadians out of work are of that sort. In difficult times Canadians should be working more, not less; work is not a luxury that we must give up when it becomes necessary to practise austerity. It's our consumption that should then be restrained, not our production. If restrictive measures applied by government – cuts in its spending, increases in taxation to cut public spending – put people out of work, they aggravate the country's difficulties by causing reduction in production when what is needed is increase.

Restraints that cause loss of jobs are particularly damaging when such loss is already occurring for other reasons. As many observers have pointed out, Canada has a problem of "structural unemployment": large numbers of jobs have been lost because traditional industries have been declining and new production modes have reduced the labour required in other industries.

Thus automobiles are now smaller and lighter, and will continue to be made with a larger proportion of plastic, ceramics, and aluminum. The automobile industry will therefore consume less steel than before. The steelmaking industry faces a permanent decline in a major market, which means fewer workers will be needed in steel mills, in iron ore and coal mines, in the transportation industries, and so on. There will be less need for oil refineries because smaller, more fuel-efficient automobiles will consume less gasoline and because better-insulated buildings will need less heating oil. Ever more sophisticated technology is eliminating traditional employments. Computers are replacing minds; robots are replacing hands. What's more, workers in newly industrializing countries are garnering a larger share of the shrinking world total of jobs.

If the reduction in jobs for Canadians caused by these developments is to be offset, then expansion must occur in other sectors of the Canadian economy. Instead of promoting such expansion, however, policies of restraint have caused contraction in those other sectors where the number of jobs might have been increased; those restraints have caused as much, or more, loss of jobs than did the structural changes going on in the economy. Canada's unemployment rate leapt from 7.5 per cent in 1981 to 11.0 per cent in 1982 not because of a sudden structural change in the Canadian economy, but primarily because of federal government tax increases and sharp escalation of interest rates by the Bank of Canada.

The Canadian economy requires major structural change if it

is to be in conformity with the changed world. A great deal of capital has to be invested in new types of public facility and new types of private enterprise. This necessary task of adjustment will be carried out more speedily, more effectively, and with far less trauma if the country is prosperous, if large amounts of finance capital are available at low rates of interest. There would then be plenty of businesses able and willing to invest in enterprises directed towards the future; there would be an abundance of jobs for workers whose present employments were extinguished by structural change. The restraints applied by our economic authorities have slowed and hindered the necessary restructuring of the Canadian economy.

Eminent businesspeople keep warning that Canada must raise the level of its industrial technology. These warnings are, of course, absolutely justified. It really is vital that we be able to manufacture innovative, sophisticated products that incorporate the latest scientific advances, that are attractively designed, competently engineered, efficiently produced, and effectively marketed. Other countries already have these abilities, and more are acquiring them. If we don't achieve these types of competence we will not be able to sell industrial products on world markets – or, for that matter, on the Canadian market.

We will be hewers of wood and drawers of water for the rest of the world, providing raw materials to the fabricating industries of other countries. For employment we will have only the work of extracting and processing natural products, not the more challenging and better-paid work of fashioning them into manufactured goods. When our natural resource endowment is exhausted, we will have no jobs at all.

If we are to be makers of sophisticated manufactured goods, we must have the necessary kinds of personnel. We will need top-notch scientists carrying on research in well-equipped laboratories, discovering facts and principles that can be applied in industrial production. We will need professionally educated engineers, together with trained and experienced technicians, persons who have picked up challenging ideas in their education and have acquired in their working experience thorough familiarity with a wide variety of materials and industrial processes. Among such people there are bound to be individuals who creatively devise attractive variants of products now being made, who conceive advantageous alterations to current production processes.

We must have as well knowledgeable, cultivated, articulate people who can locate market opportunities and sell goods effectively. Canada will achieve industrial advance only to the extent that its population contains people with these kinds of ability, training, and experience.

The economic policies currently being applied by our public authorities are the exact opposite of those needed to achieve industrial advance. Instead of fostering expansion of the country's output of appropriately qualified people, policy-makers are applying measures of contraction. Governments are tightly limiting the funding of universities, technical colleges, and public schools, obliging them to lay off staff, reduce the number of courses they offer, limit the number of students they enrol. Large numbers of applicants will be turned away from educational institutions; those who are admitted will acquire an inferior product.

Opportunity for achieving industrial advance is being grossly wasted. People who have the qualifications to impart to young people knowledge and ideas that would make them more productive members of Canada's labour force are unemployed. So are people who, if they were at work, would be thinking up new products, new production processes. So are people who could be acquiring knowledge and experience that would make them effective marketers of Canadian products. All kinds of people who could be contributing to our output of goods now and enlarging our capacity to produce and sell in the future, are idle or underemployed, frustrated and bitter.

Our authorities are applying their negative policies in order to cut their spending. Business leaders, firmly persuaded that the road to economic advance is by financial retrenchment, warmly approve. The same people who ringingly declare that Canada must improve its industrial technology urgently demand public policies that would slow down and altogether prevent such improvement.

Improvement in productivity means acquiring the ability to turn out the same output at lower cost. This achievement is gained by an increase in human skill or energy applied, by an improvement in organization, or by the introduction of more efficient equipment.

Whatever the source of the gain, one consequence always follows: less labour is needed than before to produce the same amount of output.

If the total output of the country remains the same as before, then the effect of a productivity increase will be to reduce the number of jobs in the country. The level of employment will remain the same only if a sufficient increase occurs in the country's production. But an increase in production will occur only if an increase occurs in the total amount of spending within the country. Businesses produce output in order to sell it; if there is no prospect of customers buying a larger output, businesses will not produce it.

If an increase in productivity is not accompanied by a sufficient increase in national spending, the overall effect may be negative, not positive. There would be no increase in the country's production of goods and, therefore, no improvement in its material well-being. But there would be the trauma of unemployment suffered by displaced workers – which could more than offset the additional profit achieved by the businesspeople whose firms had achieved the productivity gains.

History offers ample illustration of productivity gains that brought great distress. The introduction of mechanical looms in England in the early nineteenth century resulted in the unemployment of thousands of hand-loom weavers; the suffering lasted more than a generation. Other advances in productivity in England had similar consequences for workers. The folk memory of the English working class contains a host of bitter recollections of increases in productive efficiency that brought job loss and privation for workers. The 1984 coal strike was a furious reaction against yet another rationalization of production that imposed worker lay-offs.

This is not to say that improvements in productivity are always unwelcome and should always be opposed. They bring the possibility of a desirable increase in the country's output of goods, so that the average person becomes materially better off. They make possible the production of totally new goods that add agreeably to well-being. They make possible the elimination of jobs that are disagreeable and dangerous.

But, as sad historical experience shows, these possibilities are not necessarily realized. What is needed is economic policy that assures that workers displaced by productivity gains will not remain jobless.

Such policy is warranted on both moral and pragmatic grounds. It's an obscenity that what is hailed as "progress" should victimize innocent persons, that benefits achieved by some people are heavily offset by harm suffered by others. And there is the reality that people who face the prospect of being thrown out of work by a productivity improvement will fight to prevent it. Because of their opposition it will be introduced later, more slowly, in less effective form. And if some people wind up jobless, the country loses the output they could have produced.

Certainly Canada should aim to improve its productivity. But policies should be in place to ensure that improvement in the country's productive capability is not accompanied by the waste and frustration of unemployment. Otherwise what could be a blessing turns out to be a curse.

According to a widely held view, the Canadian economy, being so heavily dependent on international trade, especially on exports to the U.S., is susceptible to crippling blows against which it is totally helpless. That view is misguided.

Economic conditions in Canada are not absolutely determined by external forces that we have no power to control. The fact that the U.S. is in a recession does not mean that Canada is bound to have a severe unemployment problem and can expect a reduction of that problem only when economic conditions improve in the U.S. Admittedly, when the U.S. and other industrialized countries are in a recession they need less of our raw materials, leading to lay-offs in our mines and lumber mills. Lay-offs will also occur if foreign buyers turn to other sources for types of materials that we produce. And foreign-owned multinationals may close down Canadian branch plants because of poor market conditions or because they wish to relocate their operations elsewhere.

But while we are bound to suffer adverse effects from such developments we should, and could, keep the harm to a minimum. If they occur, we could allow the foreign exchange rate of the Canadian dollar to fall, thereby making all our products cheaper for foreign buyers and lowering the cost to foreign businesses of operating branch plants in Canada. We could encourage firms whose export sales are down to produce for stockpile; they would thereby keep their people working, and the goods produced could prove to be highly saleable when foreign markets recover.

The economic policies applied by Ottawa have in fact prevented such adjustments. The Bank of Canada has deliberately kept the foreign exchange rate of the Canadian dollar above its market level, making Canadian products artificially dearer to foreigners – at a time when their demand for them was already low. The high interest rates the bank imposed on the country made stockpiling prohibitively expensive.

It would be unrealistic to expect that we could salvage all the jobs lost in Canada because of recession in other countries or because of new trade barriers that they impose. Despite depreciation of our dollar, we probably still could not sell as much as before in foreign markets; even at much lower interest rates we could not keep on producing for stockpile.

But most of Canada's unemployed look for jobs in industries that produce for the domestic market, not for export. And the federal government, which could be applying policies to stimulate and expand that market, has in fact applied policies to depress and contract it.

For instance, we badly need additional apartment blocks in most of our big cities, and we have the labour and materials to build them. The Bank of Canada's policy of high interest rates has prevented the investment in new housing that would generate work for unemployed Canadians and provide us with badly needed additional accommodation.

This kind of waste and loss has not been imposed on us by world recession or higher foreign tariffs. The fact that there are fewer jobs for Canadian miners and lumberjacks, who depend on foreign demand, does not mean that construction workers who build housing for Canadians must also be out of work. Nor do Canadians have to be unemployed when they could be building needed railway lines, docks, and roads.

Different fiscal and monetary policies followed by Ottawa would have kept many Canadians at work, despite difficulties in our trade with other countries. Their recessions or tariffs imposed some harm on us from which we could not escape, but most of our economic wounds were self-inflicted.

Another frequently repeated dogma has been that foreigners could impose inescapable, severe unemployment on us by greatly raising the price of some commodity they sold us, or by withholding it altogether. This was the widely predicted consequence of the huge increase in oil prices imposed by OPEC countries in the 1970s. Experts declared that many industries would be unable to pay the greatly increased prices and would therefore be forced to shut down, throwing their employees out of work.

But there is no reason why, after an inevitable brief period of dislocation, there should not be as many jobs as ever in the country after such a price rise. Intelligent policy would concentrate great effort on reducing the country's dependence on the import whose price had soared. New techniques of production could be developed that reduced the amounts required; substitutes could be devised. Large numbers of persons would be needed to apply the new technologies, to produce the substitutes. Probably the new method of production would be less efficient than the old; the substitutes would likely be less desirable than the original. More than ever, therefore, it would be necessary to have as many people working as possible, in order to produce as much as possible and minimize the loss of well-being caused by the reduced availability of foreign products. And, as a matter of fact, the increase in oil prices did lead to a tremendous expansion of oil exploration and development activity in Canada that generated hundreds of thousands of jobs.

Ironically, the sharp decline in world oil prices that occurred after 1981 caused a huge loss of jobs in Canada, in oil exploration and related activities. The wildly escalated world price that had been declared to be disastrous for Canada turned out to be indispensable to its prosperity.

A great many people consider reduction of the federal deficit to be the country's top economic priority. And they take it for granted that there are only two ways of doing it – reduction in the federal government's spending and increase in its tax revenue. The business community generally feels that reduction in spending should be the method used; a tax increase would be burdensome to them and a deterrent to investment. Many economists, concerned that reduction in spending on public services and transfer payments would have damaging effects, favour tax increases as the means of reducing the deficit. Both types of measure would increase unemployment and reduce production in the country. Application of them will not necessarily reduce the deficit, as Canadian experience indicates. Allan MacEachen's 1981 budget contained tax increases and expenditure reductions intended to reduce the deficit; in fact, it nearly doubled in the following year.

There is another strategy available to bring down the deficit: stimulation of the economy. Lower the personal income tax to increase the public's spending power; lower the corporation profit tax to induce increase in investment; increase spending on public works, such as roads and power plants, and on public services that will increase the country's productive capability, such as training and research. Applied on a sufficient scale, such measures could restore prosperity in Canada, in the way that spending on the war effort restored prosperity during the 1940s. The government would no longer have to pay out huge sums in unemployment insurance and welfare; despite the reduction in rates of taxation, the total tax collection could go up because of the great increase in taxable income. The result of measures that bring full employment and prosperity could be reduction of the deficit.

There is, of course, no assurance of such an outcome. Even if everyone were working, the federal government might still have just as large a deficit as it has now, or even larger. However, as recent budgets have demonstrated, a strategy of economic repression might not prevent increase in the deficit either.

While a program of economic stimulation – tax reduction and expenditure increase – might fail to bring down the deficit, it would certainly put unemployed Canadians back to work and bring about increase in the country's production. Restoration of employment and increase in production would give the country a definite psychological lift.

In short, expansionist strategy to reduce the deficit is certain to produce some good results in the form of increased employment and production, but may fail to prevent an adverse result in the form of increase in the deficit. Restrictionist strategy is *certain* to do harm in the form of reduction in employment and production and may *also* fail to prevent an adverse result in the form of increase in the deficit.

Sadly, war has been the only public work that governments have financed to a sufficient degree to generate full employment. Governments have demonstrated in wartime a prodigious financial capacity far beyond what they believed they had in peacetime. Prime Minister R. B. Bennett suspended in 1932 a federal works program undertaken earlier to create jobs, on the grounds that the federal government could not afford the $27-million outlay. During the peak war years, from 1942 to 1945, the Canadian government's expenditure on the war effort averaged more than $4 billion a year, over 150 times the amount that Bennett had believed to be beyond the government's means in peacetime.

The jobs created by the production of munitions do not depend on their being actually fired in a war. Employment is generated by their production even though they are never actually used. Indeed, such has been the fate of a large part of the weaponry produced in the U.S. in the past decade or so. Many weapons serve no purpose, become obsolete as better weapons are developed, and eventually are simply scrapped. As a matter of fact, enormous effort has been applied and money spent on the development of weapons that have turned out to be absolutely useless and have never actually been produced in quantity. Nevertheless, those totally wasted expenditures also provided jobs, both directly and through spin-off effect. In Canada the development of the Avro Arrow fighter aircraft provided thousands of jobs, until Prime Minister John Diefenbaker decided to abandon the program.

Preparation for war, as opposed to actual war, has also been liberally financed and has generated jobs on a substantial scale. Fifty years ago *The Economist* of London published an article entitled "Guns to the Rescue." Its theme was that Britain's heavy spending on rearmament, prompted by the growing threat of a Nazi Germany led by Adolf Hitler, was creating jobs for workers who had long been unemployed. The production of guns was rescuing the economy from the grip of prolonged depression. Several years before, the British government had declared itself unable to finance a housing program that would have provided jobs and housing, both badly needed. Now it was spending immensely larger amounts on weapons of war and thereby generating hundreds of thousands of well-paid jobs in armament factories.

Guns came to the rescue of the U.S. economy in the 1980s. The $300-billion-a-year armament program launched by President Reagan in 1981 generated jobs on a scale sufficient to lower the country's unemployment rate from 11 per cent to 7 per cent. And, contrary to the predictions of a host of economic experts, that immense expenditure and the accompanying huge increase in the federal deficit did not bring on a wild inflation. The inflation rate actually fell after 1981, from about 14 per cent to about 4 per cent.

That result was unsurprising. With millions of unemployed

Americans back at work, it was possible for the country to have more armaments and more civilian goods as well. Inflation fell despite the increase in the deficit, because the deficit had not been the cause of the inflation problem, as alleged by a great many experts. The cause had been wage and profit increases far in excess of productivity growth. Those increases moderated after 1981, so the inflation rate declined.

The economy of the U.S. is roughly ten times as large as that of Canada. The Canadian equivalent of the U.S. spending $300 billion would be to spend $30 billion. That is how much the Canadian government would have to commit – to armaments or anything else – in order to create an impact on the Canadian economy comparable to the impact the Reagan arms program has had on the U.S. economy.

Instead, Marc Lalonde, as minister of finance, announced that the federal government would spend $1 billion on job generation in 1983. Michael Wilson, who became minister of finance in 1984, announced that the new federal administration would also spend $1 billion on job generation. Since the number of Canadians seeking work was in the neighbourhood of 1.5 million, the job generation programs announced by both Lalonde and Wilson had no visible impact; the unemployment rate remained virtually the same despite their programs.

Critics have taken the failure of these programs to lower Canada's unemployment rate appreciably as proof that the government can't solve the unemployment problem by "throwing money at it," that "we can't spend our way out of a depression." The programs have been pathetically small in scale, however, in relation both to the number of unemployed and to the U.S. program that has achieved significant reduction in that country's unemployment problem.

It's true that no adequately funded program to generate jobs for unemployed Canadians has succeeded. The reason, however, is the reason given by George Bernard Shaw for the failure of Christianity: it hasn't been tried. The Canadian government has been prepared to spend money on a scale sufficient to ensure full employment only during the catastrophe of war; in the absence of such a catastrophe we must, apparently, suffer large-scale unemployment.

Committed socialists contend that the capitalist system depends on war and preparation for war to achieve full employment. They are wrong. As Japan is demonstrating today, it is perfectly possible for a capitalist country to keep its labour force fully employed in the production of goods for peaceful use. What is needed is a national government that, when unemployment looms, undertakes needed public works and services and provides new stimuli to the country's private firms. That is what the Japanese government has been doing for many years now, thereby keeping the unemployment rate under 3 per cent. It has incurred huge budget deficits, comparable in size to those of Canada and the U.S. in the 1980s. They were financed entirely within the country and therefore created no obligations to outsiders. The performance of the Japanese economy indicates that the immense debt incurred by the Japanese government to its own people has not constituted a significant burden.

If the Canadian government spent enough on new public projects and sufficiently boosted the private sector, it could generate jobs on a very large scale, as the Reagan arms program is doing in the U.S. Canadian business leaders are adamantly opposed, however. The country's most ardent supporters of the capitalist system vehemently insist on policies that would prove socialist critics of capitalism to be right.

Finally, a myth often used as an excuse for inaction is that we do not have enough capital to cure our unemployment. Election campaign oratory in Canada traditionally includes undertakings to attract foreign capital. Those promises are irrelevant and misleading. Canada doesn't need foreign funds in order to have more jobs.

There is no shortage of capital in Canada. We are one of the richest countries in the world, and our saving rate is one of the world's highest. The reason we have a high rate of unemployment is not that Canada has insufficient financial capacity. We have high unemployment because we are not fully using the financial capacity that we possess.

During World War II there was a super-abundance of jobs in Canada. The federal government put 750,000 Canadians into uniform and employed 1.25 million in war industry. Those 2 million Canadians directly employed in the national war effort constituted one-third of Canada's labour force at the time. The labour force today is more than double what it was then; what the government did during the war was the equivalent to employing over 4 million persons in public works and public projects today. That over-full employment of wartime was achieved without five cents of foreign capital. It was achieved by drawing on purely Canadian financial capacity.

We have no less financial capacity in peacetime. The federal government could create jobs on the same scale today by spending money on public works and services, by tax reductions that enable the public to spend more on consumer goods and induce business firms to invest in new plant.

What we should get from foreigners is know-how and expertise. Americans, Japanese, Germans, and Britons have developed attractive new products and efficient new methods of production; we would like to make those products in Canada, to apply those production technologies. We can provide the necessary capital. In fact, we are already doing that for Japanese and Korean auto assembly plants. Nearly all the money needed to build those plants is being provided by Canadian governments or borrowed within Canada.

Canadian politicians and business leaders have all too often excused Canada's poor economic performance on the grounds that foreigners don't do enough for us; the major reason for the country's high unemployment rate, according to them, is that foreigners don't send us enough of their money. The excuse is feeble and groundless. Our own financial capacity is perfectly adequate to support full employment; we just haven't been using it. The credulous assumption that Canada can ever be short of Canadian dollars has prevented the government from carrying out projects that were desirable and for which we had the physical capability.

NINE

Federal Deficits—How Troublesome?

Money is like muck, not good except it be spread.
FRANCIS BACON

Since 1975 "the deficit" – the gap between the federal government's tax revenues and its expenditures – has been a matter of near-universal concern in Canada. The U.S. deficit, relatively much smaller than Canada's, has caused equally wide concern in that country and, in fact, throughout the world. In both countries federal administrations have repeatedly vowed to reduce the deficit; observers have graded their economic competence largely on the basis of how well they fulfilled that pledge. Curiously, despite steady continuation of deficits that experts warned would be absolutely ruinous, both countries have managed to survive. The sky has not fallen, as the experts predicted it would.

Everybody knows that a person or a business that keeps having deficits year after year is bound eventually to go bankrupt. A government surely is no different: it, too, must abide by the self-evident axiom that outgo cannot continually exceed income. An ordinary Canadian can't help feeling concern when the government keeps "going in the hole" by $30 billion or so a year and its already accumulated debt stands at about $200 billion. Surely this is too much, even for a national government; surely some kind of economic débâcle is bound to occur if this keeps on.

The concern felt by the ordinary citizen about federal deficits and debt, based on personal experience and common sense, is likely to be heightened by the constantly repeated, highly publicized warnings of experts. A host of politicians, pundits, businesspeople, and academics keep predicting dire consequences for the country if the federal government doesn't "get its financial house in order," "stop living beyond its means," "pouring out the red ink," and so on. As mentioned previously, commentators darkly refer to the government's annual deficits as a "ticking time bomb."

Denunciation of government debt is fortified by the sense that the reasons for it are unworthy. Ottawa, the critics charge, keeps running up these huge deficits because of its waste and mismanagement, and because vote-hungry politicians spend recklessly to curry public favour.

They point an accusing finger at the public itself: it must share some of the responsibility for those deficits. It has voted the guilty parties into office, has demanded all kinds of costly public services and hand-outs, has vehemently objected to suggestions that it should pay more in taxes. It refuses to support any aspirants to public office who promise to cut government spending and raise taxes. It threatens to vote out of office any politicians who adopt measures that would reduce the deficit – which is a very good reason why such measures are not introduced.

The critics chide the public for lacking in civic morality as well as civic responsibility. For the debt that the government is piling up will not disappear with the present generation – it will be a continuing liability of the Canadian people. Canadians yet unborn are being saddled with heavy obligations because of our waste, mismanagement, and self-indulgence. What a generation we are, passing on to our children and grandchildren a legacy of $200 billion of debt!

Not that we are escaping scot-free. We, too, the critics note, are already bearing the burden of the government's debt. A major reason why our taxes are so high now is that the government has to raise the money needed to pay its huge interest charges: in 1985 roughly a third of all its tax revenue had to go for that purpose.

What's more, the government's heavy burden of debt drastically limits its discretionary spending power. Because it has to apply so large a fraction of its revenue to the servicing of debt, the government has little money left with which to provide services that we would like to have and to undertake projects that would improve the country. After meeting its debt obligations, it simply hasn't the means to build useful additions to the country's physical structure. It cannot increase, but must rather reduce, its outlays on public services like education; it cannot undertake job creation programs for the unemployed, to anything like the extent desirable. That heavy burden of interest charges simply leaves it with no "room for manoeuvre."

Every deficit, declare the experts, causes additional forms of harm. The government's overspending of its income adds to the money in circulation, driving prices upward; big deficits have been the cause of double-digit inflation. They are responsible as well for the high interest rates that have plagued the country: the government's huge demand for funds to finance its deficits has driven interest rates sharply upward. It is because of these deficits, therefore, that home-buyers have to make higher payments on mortgages, tenants have to pay higher rents, farmers and businesspeople are driven into bankruptcy.

Big government deficits, what's more, cause reduction in private-sector investment. Businesspeople, alarmed by them and deeply concerned by the government's swelling debt burden, become afraid to expand their plant, afraid to undertake new ventures. Even if they are not held back by fear, they are deterred from borrowing by the high rates of interest that big deficits cause. And even if they are prepared to pay those steep rates, they still can't borrow because the government is taking so much of the available money that private enterprise is being "crowded out" of the country's capital markets. It is because of big federal deficits, therefore, that new commercial and industrial plant is not being built.

Tough-minded financial experts lambaste the hypocrisy of politicians who grandly promise big reductions in the deficit and then irresponsibly shrink from making the necessary major cuts in government spending, because they fear losing the votes of the many people who would be thrown out of work. (Other observers cynically note that these financial experts are, without exception, safe in their jobs; there is no possibility of their becoming unemployed themselves as a result of implementation of the measures they urge.)

Every one of the propositions laid down by the experts, solemnly declared to be axiomatic, disintegrates under even cursory examination.

First of all, the size of the deficit is always exaggerated. It is taken to be the difference between federal revenue and expenditures – with no regard for the fact that some of those expenditures are for projects and durable assets that will yield benefits and services for many years. When a private business puts up a new plant or instals new machinery to increase its capacity or improve its efficiency, it is said to be making a long-term investment. If it builds a new canteen or recreational facility, it is also considered to be making an investment, whose return will take the form of improved employee well-being and morale.

The outlays for such purposes are applauded; no objection is raised if the money to pay for them is borrowed. If, because of spending on durable assets, a firm's total expenditures in a year exceed its revenues in that year, no one declares that it is operating at a deficit. Only a portion of its total outlay is charged as current expense, attributable to the current year's operations.

Different terminology and different accounting practice are applied to basically similar operations carried out by governments. When the government builds a durable facility such as a road, school, bridge, or park, it is not deemed to be making an investment; it is only making an expenditure. So although $12 billion of the federal government's 1985 spending of $97 billion was on capital assets such as roads and buildings, the "government spending" referred to by commentators was still $97 billion. The deficit was declared to be the difference between its revenue and $97 billion. If private enterprise accounting procedures had been followed, the deficit would have been $12 billion smaller – the shortfall of revenue from $85 billion.

What's more, a considerable part of the federal government's outlays generate projects and assets that will have lasting benefit elsewhere in the Canadian economy. The grants it makes to provincial governments are used in part to finance provincial public works such as highways and bridges. The grants and subsidies it gives to private businesses enable them to build plant and acquire equipment. The tax concessions it makes to investors – which reduce its revenue and therefore increase the deficit – induce the construction of housing and commercial and industrial buildings.

The dollar figure that is declared to be the size of the federal deficit is always a grossly overstated amount; if it were calculated according to ordinary business practice, it would be very much smaller.

Common sense and the factual record both attest that federal budget deficits are not the cause of inflation and high interest rates. They will indeed have inflationary effect if they are incurred when there is full employment, when the country is producing as much as it possibly can. If at such a time the government spends more than it takes from the public by taxation, it will be adding to a national total of spending that is already sufficient. More money will chase the same amount of goods, and the price level is bound to rise.

But that is not our situation, and has not been for years. Deficits incurred when people are unemployed, when the country's productive power is not being fully used, need not have inflationary effect. The addition to spending could be matched by increase in output, leaving the price level unchanged. If, of course, the government spending is on absolutely useless projects that add nothing to national output, then it would be inflationary. But so long as additional spending serves to put unemployed people to productive work, it need not cause a rise in the price level. As demonstrated in Chapter 6, an increase in spending could even turn out to be deflationary.

The fact is that the price of anything is, broadly speaking, the aggregate of three elements: cost of materials, workers' wages, and owner's profit. The total can never be more than the sum of the three parts; if they all stay the same, there can be no increase in price. If a price goes up, it is only because one or more of these cost factors has risen. If no such increases occur in the country, then the price level will not rise, no matter how big the government's deficit is.

Within the past half-century there have been two other periods when the Canadian government incurred a series of budget deficits comparable to those of the 1980s. From 1930 to 1935, during the Great Depression, its deficits averaged 3.2 per cent of the country's gross national product and were therefore equivalent to contemporary deficits of about $15 billion. Far from there being any inflation, there was actually deflation: the consumer price index *fell* by 19 per cent, while interest rates were 3 to 4 per cent. During the war years of 1942 to 1945, the average federal deficit was 21 per cent of the gross national product, equivalent to a deficit in our time of about $100 billion. The consumer price index meanwhile rose by less than 2 per cent a year, while interest rates stayed under 4 per cent.

We have had more recent relevant experience. The federal deficit in 1985 was three times what it had been in 1981; the inflation rate, however, instead of going up, went down; in 1985 it was only a third of what it had been in 1981. Apparently if the deficit is an inflationary factor, it is only a very minor one, and its effects can be absolutely swamped by other factors, if a huge increase in its size is accompanied by a *reduction* in the country's inflation rate.

U.S. experience has exactly paralleled ours. During the 1930s, when the government had deficits comparable in size to its current ones, the price level *fell* by more than 20 per cent. During World War II, when the deficits were absolutely astronomic in size, equivalent to deficits today of over $700 billion, the inflation rate was negligible. Between 1981 and 1985, when the deficit tripled, the inflation rate declined by about three-quarters.

The federal deficit does not inevitably "crowd out" private borrowers: it will do so if there is full employment and the country's financial capacity is already being stretched to the limit. Government borrowing to finance a deficit would at such a time be competing for the same funds being sought by private enterprise; the effect would be to drive up interest rates and leave less money for private borrowers. But if the government borrows at a time when the economy is not fully employed, and when therefore its financial capacity is not fully engaged, there need be no increase in interest rates or any reduction in the amount of money that is available for private enterprise to borrow. The government will be taking from the market funds that the private sector doesn't want anyway.

A kind of teeter-totter relationship is likely to exist between private and government borrowing: the rise of one is likely to be accompanied by the descent of the other. If the private sector is buoyant and the economic outlook bright, then businesses will want to borrow a great deal in order to build all the additional plant that promises to be profitable. At such a time the government is likely to have little or no deficit, and therefore little or no need for borrowing. Its tax revenues will be bountiful and its expenditures on unemployment insurance, welfare, and job creation programs will be low.

On the other hand, when the economy is stagnant and the outlook gloomy, then the private sector will want to borrow very little while the government will have to borrow a great deal, since the inevitable reduction in tax collections, combined with larger outlays on unemployment insurance, welfare, and job creation programs, will produce a large deficit.

The enormous increase in the federal deficit has not frightened businesspeople away from investing or caused "crowding out," in either the U.S. or Canada. In the U.S., despite the near-threefold increase that occurred in the deficit between 1981 and 1984, the total of private-sector lending by commercial banks was 27 per cent higher in 1984 than it had been in 1981 and higher yet in 1985. In Canada private-sector borrowing did indeed decline between 1982 and 1983, but the reason, quite clearly, was that the country was in a recession and the business outlook was poor. Businesses, able to sell only about three-quarters of what they could produce in their existing plant, had no cause and were in no mood for expansion. They weren't "crowded out"; they didn't want to come in.

Improved economic conditions after 1983 prompted a substantial increase in bank borrowing; the amount loaned by Canada's chartered banks to the private sector was 6 per cent greater in 1984 than it had been in 1981 – despite a threefold increase in the federal deficit – and it rose again in 1985.

While the federal government was allegedly taking up so much of the available money in Canada that there was little left for private borrowers, the banks nevertheless were apparently able to extend large loans for take-overs and to borrowers who were poor credit risks. A consortium of Canadian banks loaned $4 billion in 1981 to the oil giant Dome Petroleum; the money was used to finance a wildly over-ambitious program of exploration and the take-over of another oil giant. A different consortium of Canadian banks provided the Canada Development Corporation with $2.1 billion in 1981 for the take-over of Aquitaine, a French-owned oil firm operating in Canada. An investigation into the practices of two small banks that were forced to close their doors in 1985 revealed that they had made loans – in the U.S. as well as in Canada – on very inadequate security. Several of the country's larger banks acknowledged that they had made loans totalling billions of dollars in Mexico and South American countries – and would never recover the money. The number of farm bankruptcies soared in Canada in the 1980s, in considerable part because banks had made bigger loans to farmers than were warranted.

The "crowding-out" phenomenon of the 1980s has existed only in imaginations: no Canadian bank has been unable to lend to credit-worthy firms and individuals who wanted to borrow money for reasonable purposes. The banks had the money to make all such loans – and, in addition, to finance huge take-overs and make loans to doubtful borrowers who have not repaid.

There is another kind of national deficit that is genuinely burdensome and threatening: a deficit in the balance of payments. This is the shortfall between what the Canadian nation earns from the rest of the world in a year through the sale of goods and services, and the value of the goods and services we buy from the rest of the world in that year. We make up such a deficit by borrowing foreign currency, undertaking to pay interest and repay principal in that currency. But we can earn foreigners' money only by selling them our goods and services. If, for whatever reason, we are unable to sell them very much, we will not earn the foreign currency we need to meet our debt obligations to them. In total contrast to a balance-of-payments deficit, which can be covered only by borrowing from foreigners, a federal government deficit is financed by borrowing from ourselves.

The world scene offers a dramatic contrast between the two types of deficit. Argentina, Brazil, Mexico, Peru, and Poland have had large balance-of-payments deficits in the past dozen years, which they covered by borrowing in foreign countries. Now they are unable to make interest and principal payments on the debt they piled up. Those payments are supposed to be made in foreign currency, and they have not been able to earn enough foreign currency because their exports are too small.

The Japanese government, on the other hand, has borrowed huge amounts from Japan's central bank and the Japanese people, piling up one of the world's biggest national debts, and using the money to assure full employment and the fastest possible economic growth. Whenever exports have declined, of cars, cameras, televisions, and the like, the government has quickly applied stimuli to the economy to prevent unemployment. It has reduced taxation, thereby enabling the Japanese public to buy more of these products; it has given grants to local governments for public works projects, thereby generating jobs in the construction industry and building material industries. With its tax revenue lower and its expenditures high, it has incurred huge budget deficits. These were pragmatically accepted as necessary to avoid the loss and waste of unemployment. Since they were financed entirely within the country, they imposed no burden on the nation as a whole; all debt payments would be made, in yen, to Japanese.

Our policy-makers and a good many economic commentators apparently believe that it is sound policy to go in the same direction as Argentina, Brazil, Mexico, Peru, and Poland, piling up foreign debt, but that we court disaster if we follow the route taken by Japan. Their advice corresponds to assurance that man-eating tigers are gentle pets, while cows are savage beasts that tear their victims limb from limb.

Anxious to hold down its deficits, the federal government, whether Liberal or Conservative, has limited and on occasion reduced its financial contributions to the provincial governments. The provinces have been obliged to borrow to make up the shortfall in revenue and, because interest rates were lower abroad, have done much of their borrowing in foreign countries. Ottawa politicians, whatever their stripe, declare that there is no reason why the federal government should increase its indebtedness in order to save provincial governments from having to increase theirs. Implicit in that declaration is the false assumption that it is immaterial to Canada whether the federal government obtains money by borrowing in Canada or provincial governments obtain the same amount by borrowing in foreign countries.

In fact, as we have seen, which government borrows, and where, is of enormous significance. Federal government borrowing, done within the country, does not impose a genuine burden on the people of Canada since all payments on the debt are made to themselves. Nor is it a heavy burden on the government for it has unlimited power of taxation over its Canadian creditors, together with the authority to simply create the kind of money it is obligated to pay them. A provincial government, on the other hand, even if it borrows within Canada, will owe much or all the money to persons in other provinces who are outside its tax jurisdiction, and it certainly does not have the authority to simply create money. When a provincial government borrows in a foreign country, it creates a burden for Canada: it becomes necessary for Canada to earn through exports the foreign exchange that will be needed to make the required interest payments and principal repayment.

Pontificating politicians, business leaders, and editorialists have proclaimed, as a self-evident axiom that needs no proof, that federal government deficits have been responsible for the high level of interest rates in Canada.

There is ambiguity, however, as to just which government is to be blamed. Some commentators declare the U.S. government to be the culprit. According to them, the borrowing it has to do to finance its $200-billion deficit has driven up U.S. interest rates. Because of the dominant American role in the world economy, other countries have had to raise their interest rates correspondingly. If they had failed to do so, they would have experienced large capital outflows and severe depreciation of their currencies. Because of its especially close ties with the U.S., Canada, more than any other country, has to keep its interest rates aligned with those of the U.S. So it is the U.S. deficit that is responsible for high interest rates in Canada. This is the view expressed by Prime Minister Mulroney, Gerald Bouey, and Michael Wilson.

But the same commentators have blamed the Canadian government's deficit, declaring that it is Ottawa's borrowing to finance its own $30-billion to $40-billion deficits that has driven up interest rates in Canada. This, too, has been emphasized by Michael Wilson and repeated by Prime Minister Mulroney and Gerald Bouey.

The two explanations are not compatible: they can't both be right. If the U.S. deficit is the sole cause of Canada's high interest rates, then the size of the Canadian government's deficit wouldn't matter. If Ottawa's deficit is the sole cause of the high level of Canadian interest rates, then it shouldn't matter how big the U.S. deficit is.

The claim that government deficits have been the fundamental cause of Canada's high interest rates – whichever government gets the blame – is in any case partial and misleading. The price of anything, be it a pound of butter, a house, a loan of money, is not determined by demand alone; supply is also a determinant. An increase in the demand for anything will not bring a rise in its price if it is accompanied by an equal increase in supply. As a matter of fact, an increase in demand will not bring a rise in price even if *no* increase occurs in supply – but controls exist to prohibit any rise in price. In such a case some people will be frustrated; they wind up with money in their pockets that they wanted to spend but couldn't. That is what happened, on a very large scale, during World War II. Goods were in short supply, but their prices were controlled and quantities were rationed; people saved money because it simply wasn't possible to spend it.

The supply of money in the U.S. is controlled by the Federal Reserve System's board of governors, whose chairman and dominant figure in the 1980s has been Paul Volcker. If U.S. interest rates have risen, it is not just because of an increase in demand – coming from whatever source – but also because Volcker has refused to allow a corresponding increase in the country's money supply. He has taken this line because of his conviction that such an increase in money supply would have severe inflationary effect. That view is challengeable. There were over 8 million Americans out of work when rates began their steep climb in the early 1980s. If an increase in spending served to put unemployed persons to productive work, it would not necessarily have had inflationary effect: increase in output could have matched and offset the increase in money supply and spending. And even if some inflation had occurred as a result of an increase in the money supply, it might have been acceptable; a slight increase in the inflation rate could have been a worthwhile trade-off for a large reduction in the number of unemployed in the country.

The Canadian money supply is controlled by the Bank of Canada, whose governor since the late 1970s has been Gerald Bouey. He too has applied restrictive policies, tightly limiting the country's money supply and thereby assuring that, given the demand, the rate of interest would be high. Like Volcker he believes that despite a very high unemployment rate in the country, anything beyond a very small increase in the national money supply would be inflationary. In addition, he has been concerned to hold up the foreign exchange rate of the Canadian dollar and, for that reason, feels obliged to keep Canadian interest rates in line with those of the U.S.

Contrary to incessantly repeated declaration, budget deficits, whether of the U.S. government or the Canadian government, have not been *the* cause of Canada's high interest rates. At least equal contributing causes were the highly challengeable policies applied by the monetary authorities of the two countries.

Some Canadian commentators have referred admiringly to the resolute way in which U.S. authorities propose to deal with the problem of federal government deficits. Congress passed in 1985 the so-called Gramm-Rudman law, which requires the federal government to reduce its deficit to zero by 1991. That reduction is to be achieved in equal stages over the six-year period, primarily by reductions in spending. The prospect of large cuts in federal spending has roused widespread apprehension: a great many people face the prospect of losing their jobs. Ironically, the attempt to reduce the deficit may backfire: by slowing down the economy, it may cause large reductions in tax revenues.

One feature of recent U.S. budget deficit financing has caused legitimate concern – the extent to which the deficits have been covered by borrowing from foreigners. An estimated 15 per cent of the bonds sold by the U.S. government in recent years have been purchased by non-residents. These bond sales are creating a genuine burden for the U.S. The federal government will, in the future, take money by taxation from the American people and hand it over to foreign bond-holders; it will not hand it back to the American people, as it does when it pays interest on domestically held bonds.

The large amount of U.S. government bonds acquired by foreigners reflects two primary considerations. Wealthy people in a great many countries have greater faith in the U.S. government and economy than they have in their own, and feel safer when they have their wealth in U.S. assets. Secondly, interest rates were considerably higher in the U.S. than in other countries that offered about the same degree of security and stability. Thus from 1978 to 1984, the yield on U.S. bonds was, on average, 7 per cent higher than on corresponding Swiss bonds and 3.3 per cent higher than on corresponding West German bonds. Many foreigners bought U.S. government bonds simply because of their attractive yield.

The high interest rates paid on U.S. government bonds in turn reflected the restrictive policies being applied by the country's monetary authority, the board of governors of the Federal Reserve System. The chairman of the board, Paul Volcker, insisted that the federal government's borrowing to cover its $200-billion deficits made those high interest rates inevitable. That claim is challengeable. From 1942 to 1945, during World War II, when the federal government was borrowing the equivalent of about $700 billion a year today, the interest rate on government bonds was continuously below 3 per cent.

TEN

The National Debt—How Burdensome?

*Like the watermen who advance forward
while they look backward.*
MONTAIGNE

Canada's "national debt" is the total owed by the federal government
to its bond-holders. The amount has soared in the past dozen years
as the government sold bonds to get the money needed to cover its
huge deficits. With high interest rates and the enormous size of the
debt, the annual interest charges are now many billions of dollars
and require a large part of the government's revenue. The people
who express concern about the national debt, however, fail to recognize its unique nature and the unique powers of the institution
that owes it. The national debt is like no other debt, and the federal
government is like no other debtor.

About 90 per cent of the government's bonds have been sold in
Canada, some to the Bank of Canada and the rest to private Canadian
firms and individuals. The government wholly owns the Bank of
Canada and has two powers possessed by no one else in the
country – unlimited power of taxation over all Canadians, and the
authority to simply create Canadian dollars in any amount. Possessed
of these powers, it can never be unable to pay Canadian creditors,
no matter how much it owes them.

In the case of bond-holders who are taxpayers, the government
takes money from their left-hand pockets in taxation in order to put
it into their right-hand pockets as bond interest. Insofar as taxpayers
and bond-holders are different persons, the government transfers
money from some Canadians to other Canadians. The real extent
of this transfer is much obscured and reduced by the fact that most
of the bonds not owned by private individuals are owned by financial
institutions – banks, credit unions, insurance companies, pension funds.

So anyone who has a bank or credit union account, holds an insurance policy, or is on a pension plan is indirectly receiving interest on federal government bonds. There are very few Canadians, consequently, who do not receive, directly or indirectly, some of the interest that the federal government pays on its bonds.

The fact that Canada in 1985 had a national debt of approximately $200 billion, on which the interest due was about $26 billion, could be represented by the following sentence: "We, the people of Canada, owe ourselves nearly $200 billion and undertake to pay ourselves nearly $26 billion as interest on that debt." There is *no* parallel here with any other kind of debt – of an individual, a private firm, a municipal or provincial government. In the case of all such debts borrower and lender are not one and the same. Individuals and businesses borrow from banks and make interest payments and principal repayments to those banks. Provincial governments borrow by selling their bonds, entirely or almost entirely, to persons who live outside their jurisdictions, and they make all payments to those persons; the community from which the government takes the money to pay its debt obligations is not the community to which it makes the payments. The same is true of borrowing by municipal governments; they, too, borrow from outsiders and make all payments on debt to those outsiders. It is only in the case of federal government borrowing, *within the country*, that the money to meet the government's debt obligations is paid to the community from which that money has been taken by taxation. Equally important, when the federal government borrows from Canadians it has the power to simply create money of the kind that it must pay its creditors. No provincial or municipal government has that power.

When the federal government borrows money in a foreign country and undertakes to make payment in the currency of that country, then the case is totally different. This is genuine debt that is like the debt of private individuals, for it is owed to someone other than the borrower and, as well, it must be paid in a currency that the government cannot obtain by taxation or simply create. The portion of Canada's national debt owed to foreigners is only about 10 per cent, of which roughly half – about 5 per cent of the total debt – is payable in foreign currency. The other 5 per cent consists of ordinary Government of Canada bonds that foreigners have bought and on which the interest and principal are payable in Canadian dollars.

The existence of the national debt does involve some costs for

Canada, of course. The 10 per cent that is owed to foreigners is certainly a burden, especially the 5 per cent on which interest and principal payments must be made in foreign currency. Canada incurs some costs, however, even on account of the 90 per cent of the national debt that is owed within the country, on which all payments are made to Canadians, and in Canadian dollars.

An enormous amount of paper-shuffling is involved. The printing and selling of bonds, the mailing of interest payments, and the keeping of records require effort that costs millions of dollars each year. Because the government needs the money to make those interest payments, it collects a larger amount of tax than it would otherwise do; it therefore spends more on the mechanics of tax collection. The country's output is likely to be somewhat smaller than it might be, because higher taxes cause some people to work less. A transfer of income occurs from some Canadians to other Canadians, insofar as some taxpayers own few Government of Canada bonds and some bond-holders pay little federal tax. That transfer may be contrary to the national interest.

All these costs are relatively trivial, however. They are to be counted in the millions, not the billions; they are a far smaller burden on Canada than is the 5 per cent of the national debt that is owed to foreigners and payable in foreign currency.

One element in the overstatement of the burden of the national debt is simply ridiculous. The Bank of Canada, our central bank, is by far the largest single buyer of federal government bonds. In 1985 it held nearly $16 billion worth, about 7 per cent of the total then outstanding.

The Bank of Canada, being wholly owned by the federal government, turns over its net revenue to the government at the end of each calendar year. In 1985 it received $2,027 million as interest on the federal bonds it held; deducting its operating cost of $147 million, it handed over $1,880 million to the federal government at year's end. The government therefore got back more than 92 per cent of the money it had paid as bond interest to the Bank of Canada in 1985. The $2,027 million that the government paid the Bank of Canada is counted, however, *in its entirety*, as part of the government's financial burden, which must be borne by Canadian taxpayers. No regard is had for the fact that the government got practically all of it back. This kind of reckoning is ludicrous. It's equivalent to someone paying $100 for an article, getting a $90 rebate – but nevertheless insisting that it cost $100.

The people who express alarm at the size of the national debt, and the interest payments that the government must make on it, look at only one side of the coin. They don't see that for the Canadians who own the bonds, the debt is an asset and the interest payments are income. A good many of the people who express concern about the public debt refer glowingly in other contexts to the wealth and income of the people of Canada. They fail to recognize that the government liabilities and interest payments that they deplore are the private assets and interest receipts that they applaud.

Because federal government bonds are absolutely secure assets, with no possibility of default, many businesses and members of the general public are eager to keep much of their wealth and savings in this form. Ironically, therefore, if the government were ever to pay off a large fraction of its debt, the consequences would be chaotic for a great many businesses and ordinary people. They would no longer be able to purchase a financial asset that was absolutely safe. They would have to put their money into investments that were not ironclad, hoping that they had guessed correctly. Insurance companies that guessed wrong would be unable to pay policy-holders. Pension funds that made bad guesses would be unable to pay pensioners.

The national debt is not a heavy burden that we are passing on to future generations of Canadians. Posterity will indeed inherit the obligation to make huge interest payments on the national debt, but it will also inherit the bonds on which that interest is paid. What is being passed on to posterity is the obligation to tax itself in order to pay itself interest on the bonds it has inherited. That is not a crushing burden – as the factual record attests. During World War II the government borrowed the equivalent of about $100 billion a year today to finance the war effort; it was the spending of that immense amount of borrowed money that ended the Great Depression of the 1930s, replacing it with wartime prosperity. When the war ended, the national debt was nearly four times what it had been in 1939; at more than 150 per cent of the gross national product, it was the equivalent of a debt today of about $800 billion.

Experts direly predicted at the time that the post-war generation would be crushed by the burden of debt being passed on to it. Few predictions have proven to be more false. The quarter-century between 1945 and 1970 was the most prosperous in Canada's history; the generation that came to maturity in that period enjoyed a far higher standard of living and had far better opportunity than any previous generation.

Financial experts drive home the significance of Canada's national debt by this striking representation: it amounted in 1985 to $8,000 for every man, woman, and child in the country. Some experts add a note of pathos by observing that every child born in Canada is saddled with $8,000 of debt immediately on its entry into the world.

That figure of $8,000 is certainly large and daunting. Its significance becomes totally transformed, however, when it is compared with the corresponding figures of other countries. In 1985 the national debts of Pakistan and India amounted to slightly less than $200 Canadian per capita; the national debt of Zimbabwe was a little more than $200 Canadian per capita. If indeed a national debt is the heavy burden that it is proclaimed to be, then the average Canadian, carrying a debt load about forty times as great as that carried by the average Pakistani, Indian, or Zimbabwean, must be in far worse economic condition. A child that has the misfortune to be born in Canada is heavily weighted down by a type of burden that is far lighter for the children who have the better fortune to be born in Pakistan, India, or Zimbabwe.

Financial calculations that point to such conclusions are, to put it mildly, preposterous. The doomsayers totally overlook the fact that while the average Canadian is taxed to pay the interest on $8,000 of Government of Canada bonds, the same average Canadian, being the owner of nearly $8,000 of those bonds, receives that money as his due. Nor do these doomsayers have regard for the fact that each newborn Canadian infant, for whom they express concern because it is saddled with $8,000 of national debt, is also the blessed heir to about $8,000 of federal government bonds.

Comparison of Canada's national debt today with that of other countries reinforces the conclusion that follows from a comparison of Canada's national debt today with our debt in the past. So long as we borrow the money from ourselves, the size and growth of the national debt have little adverse effect, if any, on the country's economic performance.

The bottom line of a country's economic performance is the material well-being of its people, and the real significance of any economic development depends on how it affects that well-being. If something is a serious burden on Canada, then increase in its size should be accompanied by a deterioration in the well-being of the Canadian people. Huge increase in the national debt has in fact been accompanied by enormous improvement in the Canadian standard of living. The national debt soared from $5 billion in 1939 to over $200 billion in 1985, a more than fortyfold increase. The interest paid on the debt was $26 billion in 1985, nearly 200 times the $135-million figure of 1939.

Dollars paid out in 1985 did not, of course, have the same significance as dollars paid out in 1939. Because of inflation, a 1985 dollar had only about one-eighth the buying power of a 1939 dollar. The $200-billion national debt of 1985 was therefore equivalent to a 1939 figure of $25 billion, and the 1985 interest payment on debt of $26 billion was equivalent to a 1939 figure of $3.3 billion. Canada's population in 1985 was slightly more than double what it had been in 1939. If allowance is made for inflation and population growth, the figures for the federal government's debt and interest charges on debt become very much reduced; but on a per-capita basis and in "real terms," the national debt was still, in 1985, two and a half times what it had been in 1939, and the interest payment on that debt was over twelve times what it had been in 1939.

Nevertheless, the material well-being of the Canadian nation in 1985 was far greater than it had been in 1939. People were better fed, had more ample wardrobes, were more spaciously and attractively housed, worked shorter hours, had longer vacations, owned more cars and labour-saving appliances; the government provided a far larger array, and better quality, of public services. Just how serious is an alleged economic burden when a twelvefold increase in its size does not prevent the kind of improvement in well-being that Canadians have enjoyed in the past half-century?

So long as we borrow the money from ourselves, the size and growth of the national debt have little adverse effect, if any, on the country's well-being. Our actual production of goods is determined by how hard and skilfully we work, how effectively we use our natural resources, how thoroughly we apply modern technology. The amount of our output that we can have for ourselves depends on how much must be given to foreigners because they sold us products or loaned us money. The amount of goods that we have for ourselves determines the national level of material well-being; it is little affected by the scale on which we take money from ourselves in taxation and pay it to ourselves as bond interest.

Alexander Hamilton, the first secretary of the U.S. treasury, noted how advantageous it would be for the nation to finance necessary public works by borrowing from itself: the money simply could not be raised by taxation, or only with severe adverse effect; no obligation to foreigners would be incurred. Recognizing that the term "national debt" would cause concern, he suggested that it should be called the "national blessing" instead.

It is a terrible pity that his suggestion was not adopted; we might have been spared the enormous economic waste and psychological distress that has been caused by large-scale unemployment. What has been labelled "national debt" has been deemed to be, self-evidently, burdensome and threatening and therefore to be avoided at all costs. To damn any proposal for putting unemployed people to work on useful public projects, it has only been necessary to point out that it would increase the national debt and therefore impose upon the nation the obligation to make larger interest payments. It has been considered pointless and irrelevant to note that if the borrowing were done within the country, the nation would owe the money to itself and make all interest payments to itself.

Criticizing deficits is not an invention of the twentieth century. Lord Thomas Macaulay, in his *History of England* published over a century ago, had this to say about the growth of the English national debt:

> At every stage in the growth of that debt the nation has set up the same cry of anguish and despair. At every stage in the growth of that debt it has been seriously asserted by wise men that bankruptcy and ruin were at hand. Yet still the debt went on growing; and still bankruptcy and ruin were as

remote as ever. . . . [When the debt reached £140 million]
David Hume, undoubtedly one of the most profound political
economists of his time, declared that our madness had exceeded the madness of the Crusaders. Richard Coeur de Lion
and Saint Lewis had not gone in the face of mathematical
demonstration. It was impossible to prove by figures that the
road to Paradise did not lie through the Holy Land: but it
was possible to prove by figures that the road to national ruin
was through the national debt. It was idle, however, now
to talk about the road: we had done with the road: we had
reached the goal: all was over: all the revenues of the island
north of Trent and west of Reading were mortgaged. Better
for us to have been conquered by Prussia or Austria than
to be saddled with the interest of a hundred and forty millions. And yet this great philosopher – for such he was –
had only to open his eyes, and to see improvement all around
him, cities increasing, cultivation extending, marts too small
for the crowds of buyers and sellers, harbours insufficient
to contain the shipping, artificial rivers joining the chief in-
land seats of industry to the chief sea-ports, streets better
lighted, houses better furnished, richer wares exposed to sale
in statelier shops, swifter carriages rolling along smoother
roads. He had indeed only to compare the Edinburg of his
boyhood with the Edinburg of his old age. His prediction
remains to posterity, a memorable instance of the weakness
from which the strongest minds are not exempt. . . .

The attempt to lay a portion of the load on the American
colonies produced another war [1775]. That war left us with
an additional hundred millions of debt, and without the
colonies whose help had been represented as indispensable.
Again England was given over; and again the strange patient
insisted on becoming stronger and more blooming in spite
of the diagnostics and prognostics of State physicians. As she
had been visibly more prosperous with a debt of a hundred
and forty millions than with a debt of fifty millions, so
she was visibly more prosperous with a debt of two hundred
and forty millions than with a debt of a hundred and forty
millions. Soon, however, the wars which sprang from the
French Revolution, and which far exceeded in cost any that
the world had ever seen, tasked the powers of public credit to

the utmost. When the world was again at rest the funded debt of England amounted to eight hundred millions. . . . [But] after a few years of exhaustion, England recovered itself. Yet, like Addison's valetudinarian, who continued to whimper that he was dying of consumption till he became so fat that he was shamed into silence, she went on complaining that she was sunk in poverty till her wealth showed itself by tokens which made her complaints ridiculous. The beggared, the bankrupt society, not only proved able to meet all its obligations, but, while meeting those obligations, grew richer and richer so fast that the growth could almost be discerned by the eye. In every county we saw wastes recently turned into gardens; in every city, we saw new streets and squares and markets, more brilliant lamps, more abundant supplies of water: in the suburbs of every great seat of industry we saw villas multiplying fast, each imbosomed in its gay little paradise of lilacs and roses. While shallow politicians were repeating that the energies of the people were borne down by the weight of the public burdens, the first journey was performed by steam on a railway. Soon the island was intersected by railways. A sum exceeding the whole amount of the national debt at the end of the American war was, in a few years, voluntarily expended by this ruined people in viaducts, tunnels, embankments, bridges, stations, engines. . . .

The prophets of evil were under a double delusion. They erroneously imagined that there was an exact analogy between the case of an individual who is in debt to another individual and the case of a society which is in debt to a part of itself; and this analogy led them into endless mistakes about the effect of a system of funding. They were under an error not less serious touching the resources of the country. They made no allowance for the effect produced by the incessant progress of every man to get on in life. They saw the debt grow; and they forgot that other things grew as well as the debt.

The growth of Canada's national debt has generated its own long series of unfulfilled predictions of disaster. Like the promise of the English pub sign "Free Beer Tomorrow," the disaster has always been something that will take place in the future; it has never actually occurred. For over half a century financial experts have been declaring that if Canada's national debt rises any further, the country will be ruined.

During the Great Depression of the 1930s the federal government incurred a series of deficits that caused great concern. Because of the borrowing to cover those deficits, the national debt increased from $3.5 billion in 1930 to $4.8 billion in 1938. Experts warned that this huge increase in the national debt was imposing a crippling financial burden on the country in the form of the enormous interest payments to which the government was obligating itself. In 1932, in fact, the government, not daring to borrow the $27 million that would have had to be spent, cancelled a public works program it had undertaken in order to create jobs.

During World War II, the government borrowed more than $13 billion to pay for the war effort, increasing the national debt from $5 billion in 1939 to $18 billion in 1945. Experts warned that the country would be impoverished by this enormous burden of debt it had piled up.

In 1978, when the country's unemployment rate was 8.4 per cent, a figure then regarded as intolerably high, the Economic Council of Canada recommended that the federal government spend $2 billion to generate jobs. Jean Chrétien, the minister of finance, brusquely dismissed the proposal as irresponsible. For the national debt was then $63 billion and the prospect was that the government would have a deficit of $7 billion that year. Financial experts warmly commended Chrétien; the country would be crippled, they declared, if the national debt rose above $70 billion.

In 1979, during his brief tenure as minister of finance, John Crosbie emphasized that with the national debt already amounting to $82 billion, further increase would bring disaster. He therefore introduced a budget designed to eventually eliminate the deficit, the budget that was responsible for the defeat of the Clark government.

Allan MacEachen, the next minister of finance, warned in 1981 that with the national debt already at $94 billion, further increase would be calamitous. He therefore introduced a budget designed to reduce the deficit from $13 billion to $10 billion. Largely as a consequence of that budget, the economy experienced a sharp recession in 1982 and, ironically, the deficit shot up to $23 billion.

In his financial statement of November 8, 1984, Michael Wilson warned that if the government's deficits continued at their current $35-billion level, the national debt would amount to $400 billion in the year 1990. That would be absolutely catastrophic, in his view. Ottawa's interest payments on the debt would be about $50 billion, requiring half its total revenues and leaving it with insufficient funds to carry out its normal responsibilities. To ward off disaster Wilson announced spending cuts of $3.5 billion and revenue increases totalling $700 million, in order to achieve an immediate deficit reduction of $4.2 billion. And he made clear that this was only a beginning; he promised additional cuts in spending and taxation increases that would reduce the deficit further. Leaders of the business community urged that the reduction in the deficit, to be achieved primarily by cuts in government spending, be in the order of $7 billion to $8 billion.

The implications of all this were intriguing. If Wilson did manage to reduce the deficit by $8 billion a year, Canada's debt would still amount to $400 billion – but in 1995 rather than in 1990. If a $400-billion national debt means disaster, then even if Wilson did what the business community demanded of him, Canada would still not make it to the twenty-first century.

ELEVEN

Raising Interest Rates—How Helpful?

The remedy is worse than the disease.
FRANCIS BACON

In the nineteen years before 1966, the prime rate charged by the chartered banks could not legally be above 6 per cent; mortgage interest rates ranged between 4.5 and 7.5 per cent. In the nineteen years after 1966, when the ceiling was abolished, the interest rate charged by the chartered banks soared to a peak of 22.75 per cent, and mortgage interest rates were at one time above 21 per cent.

Five main justifications are given by monetary authorities and financial experts for this wild escalation:
- High interest rates combat inflation by deterring borrowing. They thereby prevent the spending of money that would have been borrowed; by holding down spending in the country, they reduce inflationary pressure.
- High interest rates are needed, during a time of inflation, to provide lenders an adequate "real" return on loans they make.
- High interest rates are needed to attract foreign capital and prevent the outflow of domestic capital.
- High interest rates are needed to strengthen the Canadian dollar, thereby keeping the Canadian economy strong.
- High interest rates combat inflation in another way as well; by keeping up the foreign exchange rate of the Canadian dollar, they hold down the price that Canadians must pay for imports.

Each one of these rationalizations is largely – or wholly – false.

The deterrent effect

High interest rates may deter borrowing only a little or not at all. A person who considers it absolutely necessary to buy a house or car will pay virtually whatever interest lenders demand for the money needed to make the purchase. As well, a person who believes that prices are going to rise sharply in the future will want to buy now, almost regardless of what interest rate must be paid to get the money. Similarly, a person who expects that the interest rate will rise may borrow now, however high the rate, to avoid the even higher rate in prospect. Someone who expects a higher income in the future will be willing to take on the obligations of large interest payments. And, finally, our perception of a rate as being high or low depends on what we have become accustomed to. In the 1940s and 1950s, when the going interest rate on mortgages was about 5 per cent, a prospective house-buyer might have regarded a 7-per-cent rate as extortionate and refused to buy if the mortgage was to be at that rate. From 1980 to 1982, when mortgage rates were over 20 per cent, anyone who offered to lend at 15 per cent would have been swamped by people eager to get in on the bargain.

What is true for individuals is equally true for businesses. A firm that badly needs new equipment or plant, or whose managers believe prices or interest rates are going to rise, will borrow to make its investment, with little regard for the interest rate it has to pay. So will a firm whose interest charges are only a small fraction of its costs: even a sharp rise in the rate of interest would add only slightly to total operating costs and therefore have little effect on investment decisions. In short, there are a great many circumstances in which high interest rates will have relatively little deterrent effect on borrowing.

The claim that increase in interest rates causes a proportionate reduction in borrowing is refuted by actual experience as well as common sense. While the prime interest rate charged by banks rose nearly fourfold between 1966 and 1981, the amount of loans they made rose from $10 billion to $90 billion. During that same period, when the mortgage interest rate tripled, the number of mortgages taken out increased from 134,000 to 178,000.

The steep interest rates of 1981 no doubt discouraged some people from taking out bank loans, from taking on mortgages. It's obvious from the figures, however, that a great many people were not deterred. For those people, the rise in interest rates constituted an additional inflationary factor. Because of higher prices, their interest payments would have been higher even if the interest rate had remained the same; they would have had to pay more in interest charges because of the larger amount they had borrowed. Increase in the rate of interest added yet more to the monthly payments they had to make. The buyer of a modest three-bedroom house in a large city in 1981 had to make monthly mortgage payments that were at least $600 more than they would have been at 1966 interest rates. The tenant in an average one-bedroom apartment in a new block in a large city had to pay at least $250 more rent per month than he would have had to pay if the builder had been able to get a mortgage at the 1966 rate. The cost of doing business increased because of the higher interest charges on borrowed money; businesses raised their prices to cover their cost increases, giving another upward push to the cost of living.

Canada's inflation rate in 1981 was the highest in thirty-three years; the steep increase in interest rates was probably a contributory factor. Certainly, the decline in interest rates from the peak levels attained in 1981 was accompanied by a decline in the inflation rate.

Insofar as high interest rates did deter families from buying new houses, builders from putting up apartment blocks, industrialists from adding to their plant, they caused unemployment in the present and contributed to inflation in the future. Workers who would have been employed in construction were idle instead, living off savings, unemployment insurance, or welfare instead of earning wages and salaries. Through spin-off effect other workers, too, lost their jobs, in industries that supplied materials and services needed in construction, in industries that catered to the demands of construction workers.

The fact that houses and apartment blocks were not built meant that, because of the smaller supply, house prices and apartment rents would be higher in the future. We are experiencing today these inflationary consequences of the high interest rates that prevailed in the past. House prices and apartment rents are unquestionably higher today than they would be if our cities and towns had the houses and apartment blocks that could have been built in the past. People who are poorly accommodated today could be living in good new housing that could have been built but wasn't. Today's rent controls would not be necessary if there were a greater supply of housing in existence; there would be a greater supply if the construction of houses and apartment blocks had not been deterred by high interest rates. Because factory buildings were not built, the supply of factory space today is smaller, and its price is therefore higher than it would have been. Fewer products are being turned out because there are fewer factories; their prices are therefore higher and the public has less of them.

In addition to deterring the construction of housing and plant that would have been welcome additions, high interest rates had a catastrophic effect on some operating enterprises. Businesses that had borrowed money when interest rates were low became obligated to pay hugely increased interest charges when interest rates escalated. A good many were simply unable to pay and had to declare bankruptcy; such was the fate of farmers who had borrowed to buy land and machinery when interest rates were low and those loans seemed perfectly reasonable.

In addition to the cost increases and output reductions that high interest rates cause directly and obviously, there are additional adverse effects that they cause indirectly, as became evident during the early 1980s. Because of heavy financing costs, businesses carried much smaller inventories; manufacturers kept on hand smaller stocks of materials; wholesalers kept less merchandise in their warehouses; retailers had fewer goods on their shelves.

As a result, manufacturers had to interrupt operations more often because they ran out of critical materials; wholesalers were not able to supply merchants as promptly as before with all the items they needed; customers in retail stores had narrower selections from which to choose and had to wait a long time for some items that they wanted.

Because they bought goods in smaller quantity, merchants lost the savings available through bulk purchase. Because what they bought was delivered in smaller quantities, they incurred higher transportation charges. Because they generally carried smaller stocks, competition among sellers was less keen.

The housing industry offered a very good illustration of the pernicious indirect effects of high interest rates. Builders didn't put up large numbers of houses. They built just a few houses at a time, only the number they were confident they could sell promptly. Construction costs were consequently higher, since builders lost economies of scale. Because only a small number of new houses were on the market at one time, customers had a more limited selection from which to choose. Because each builder built only what was sure to sell, competition among builders was less keen; buyers were not as eagerly courted as they had been when builders had large numbers of new houses for sale.

The "real" return to lenders

There is no basis to the contention that savers will refuse to lend their money if the interest rate they are offered is not well above the inflation rate, giving them a sizeable "real" return. Savers who decline to lend out their money and keep it in cash get a return of zero; any rate of interest, no matter how low, is bound to be more than that, no matter how high the inflation rate is.

The foremost concern of anyone who has savings is to not lose them. Interest on a financial asset that can be bought with savings is welcome, but of more importance is assurance that the money paid for that asset will not be lost. A very large number of Canadian savers buy Government of Canada bonds and keep their money in savings deposits guaranteed by a federal government agency. They accept whatever interest rate is paid on these bonds and deposits because they are not prepared to keep their savings in any other form, since any other form involves risk that their money will be lost. Insurance companies and pension funds, their first and foremost concern being security of their assets, invest a large proportion of their funds in federal government bonds as a matter of course.

The factual record confirms common sense. There have been a number of years when the interest rate on government bonds was lower than the inflation rate. That was the case from 1946 to 1950 and again in 1974 and 1975. Despite the fact that the "real" return on them was negative, the government had no difficulty selling its bonds in those years, to the Bank of Canada and to businesses and individuals who were not prepared to risk their money in the slightest degree. And the chartered banks received large savings deposits in those years, even though the interest they paid was lower than the inflation rate.

Since 1975 the Bank of Canada has kept the interest rate above the inflation rate, in order that lenders may get a "real" rate of return. Those high interest rates raised the cost of living by increasing the monthly payments of house-buyers and the rents of apartment tenants, by imposing on businesses an additional cost that they would pass on to customers. The Bank aggravated the country's inflation problem in order to provide savers with a rate of return higher than what would have been acceptable to them.

The real rate of return on long-term loans became grotesquely high as the inflation rate receded, while the interest paid on them remained at the levels previously contracted. In 1985, when the inflation rate was down to about 4 per cent, the federal government was still paying 18 per cent on ten-year bonds that it had issued in 1981. House-buyers who had taken out five-year mortgages between 1980 and 1982 paid even higher real rates of interest than the 14 per cent being paid by the federal government.

Foreign capital

Because foreign money that comes to Canada is always called "capital," the impression is given that it is all used to finance the construction of factories, the digging of mines, the drilling of oil wells. In fact, a large proportion of that foreign money is used to pay for imported Cadillacs and Hondas, for vacations in Hawaii, Florida, and California. Raising Canadian interest rates to attract "foreign capital" results in our borrowing from foreigners, at high rates of interest, to pay for imported consumer goods, many of which we could have produced ourselves. Thanks to terminological humbug, we become saddled with heavy debt obligations to foreigners that bring no increase in the productive power of the Canadian economy and cause actual harm. We have in recent years borrowed large amounts of money from Japan; in effect we have been borrowing the means to buy its Toyotas, Hondas, and Datsuns while Canadian employees of GM, Ford, and Chrysler plants have been laid off because of slow sales. Future generations of Canadians will be burdened by the foreign debt we are incurring in order to buy abroad what we could produce at home.

The U.S. has been doing the same thing as we. High American interest rates have attracted immense amounts of foreign funds; the U.S. has been using a large part of that foreign money to buy foreign steel and foreign automobiles – while thousands of its own steel workers and autoworkers were unemployed.

And, in a final irony, an increase in the Canadian interest rate may attract very little, if any, foreign money. All lenders want assurance, first and foremost, that they will get their money back; the promise of a high rate of interest will not attract them if there is a high risk of losing their capital. When foreigners buy the bonds of Canadian businesses or government bodies, they are exposed to such risk, for two distinct reasons. First, the borrower, unless it is the federal government, may be unable to make the payment promised; in that case all lenders, whether foreign or domestic, lose their money. Secondly, the foreign exchange rate of the Canadian dollar may fall, so that while the borrower makes all the payments promised, they are worth less to foreigners. Thus Americans who bought ten-year $100 Government of Canada bonds in May 1975 would have paid $103 in U.S. funds, because the Canadian dollar was at a 3-cent premium at that time. In 1985, however, when the bonds fell due, the $100 Canadian that the Canadian government paid them was worth only $74 in U.S. funds. Presumably if they had anticipated that they would get back only $74 of their $103 capital, they would never have bought the bonds.

A higher rate of interest offered by Canadians will not attract foreign funds if it is accompanied by the prospect that the foreign exchange rate of the Canadian dollar will be lower in the future. Ironically, higher rates of interest make that prospect more likely. For they may deter investment in the industrial plant that is needed to maintain the productive power of the Canadian economy. Our ability to export may decline and our dependence on imports may increase, making the dollar a weaker currency in the future, with a lower foreign exchange rate.

Strengthening the dollar

A "strong" dollar – that is, a dollar whose foreign exchange rate is high – is certainly desirable, but only if its high price derives from the strength of the national economy. The Japanese yen is a strong currency for sound economic reasons: Japan produces quality goods, which it sells at attractive prices. The rest of the world wants to buy enormous quantities of those goods and therefore needs immense amounts of Japanese money with which to pay. Meanwhile, Japan limits its purchases from the rest of the world so that foreigners don't earn much of its currency. The limited supply of yen available to foreigners, together with the large worldwide demand for yen, is responsible for the yen's high value.

The case of Canada has been very different. Canadians want to spend a great deal in foreign countries – on consumer goods, raw materials, machinery, vacations, and so on; in addition they have to pay interest and dividends to foreigners on their huge loans and investments in Canada. The amount of Canadian currency being offered on world markets is therefore very large. The world, however, wants relatively less of our products and needs relatively few Canadian dollars with which to pay for purchases. As well, because of our lacklustre prospects, foreigners are less enthusiastic than they once were about investing in Canada, so they need fewer Canadian dollars to pay for the digging of mines, the drilling of oil wells, the construction of factories. The combination of large supply and weak demand has caused the dollar to decline on the world's money markets.

It has fallen, however, by much less than is warranted by the demand–supply situation. For the Bank of Canada, partly to keep the dollar "strong," has raised interest rates in Canada to levels that attract large amounts of foreign funds. Foreigners buy Canadian securities that pay much higher interest rates than comparable securities in their own countries. At the same time Canadian borrowers – businesses, provincial and municipal governments – borrow in foreign capital markets, where interest rates are lower than in Canada. It is this inflow of foreign money, sent in by foreigners and brought in by Canadians, that has bolstered the foreign exchange rate of the dollar and made it appear "strong." But whereas Japan has a strong currency because it is earning large amounts from foreign buyers, we have a strong currency because we are *borrowing* large amounts from foreigners. The contrast is like the difference between someone who has an impressive amount of money because she earns a big paycheque and someone who has an impressive amount of money because he has made a big loan from the bank.

A policy of keeping the dollar strong has severely damaged important sectors of the Canadian economy. Exporters whose production costs rose substantially in the 1970s needed correspondingly higher selling prices; if, however, they raised their prices on world markets by as much as was warranted by their cost increases, they would have priced themselves out of those markets. A decline in the Canadian dollar's foreign exchange rate would have enabled them to cover their higher costs and still sell at competitive prices in world markets. In preventing such a decline, the Bank of Canada prevented the adjustment through which market forces would have enabled Canadian exporters to stay competitive on world markets despite the large increase in their production costs.

In a parallel way the Bank's intervention has harmed Canadian firms that are exposed to foreign competition. Their costs, too, rose substantially in the 1970s and they had to raise their prices accordingly. Had the Canadian dollar been allowed to depreciate to the full extent that was warranted by Canada's inflation, the cost to Canadians of foreign goods would have risen by the same degree. Because depreciation to that extent was not allowed, the cost to Canadians of foreign goods rose less than the price of equivalent domestic goods. The prices of foreign cars rose less than the prices of Canadian cars; the cost of holidays abroad rose less than the cost of holidays at home. Naturally, Canadian car-makers sold fewer cars; Canadian resort operators received fewer vacationers.

During the Great Depression of the 1930s, a number of countries were accused of following "beggar-my-neighbour" policies by "exporting unemployment" – creating jobs for their own people at the expense of workers in other countries. The primary tactic used to export unemployment was deliberate reduction of the foreign exchange rate of the national currency. By exchange rate depreciation, a country gained a competitive advantage over every other country that maintained its currency at the same exchange rate.

The advantage was twofold. Every product of the country was made cheaper to foreign buyers, who would therefore buy more. The increase in exports would generate additional jobs in the country's export industries. All foreign goods, on the other hand, were made dearer. People would buy less of them, switching to domestically produced goods that were substitutes. Firms producing such goods would take on additional workers to satisfy the larger demand.

All the additional jobs that came into being in the country that had devalued its currency would be at the expense of workers in other countries. The output of goods and the total number of jobs in the world remaining the same, other countries lost the jobs that were gained by the country that had depreciated its currency. Hence the bitter resentment against governments that depreciated their national currencies to export their unemployment.

By artificially *raising* the foreign exchange rate of the dollar above its market level, the Bank of Canada has been *importing* unemployment. All this country's goods have been made dearer to foreigners, causing reduction in exports; foreign goods have been made artificially cheaper, inducing people to buy them in preference to domestically produced equivalents. Jobs have been lost in Canada's export industries and in the industries that compete against imports. Other countries have benefited as employment has increased in their export industries.

During the early 1980s many Canadians, while concerned at

our dollar's decline in relation to the U.S. dollar, took comfort that it rose sharply against the British pound, the French franc, the German mark, and the Italian lira. The people who drew satisfaction from this rise generally overlooked the reason for it. European monetary authorities refused to follow American interest rates on their upward course. A wide gap therefore developed between the levels of European and American rates. Europeans with money to invest consequently sent very large amounts to the U.S. to take advantage of the higher returns obtainable there. Notably they bought large quantities of U.S. federal government bonds, because they paid a much higher interest rate than the bonds issued by their own governments. It was this heavy outflow of funds from European countries that pulled down the exchange rates of their currencies.

Canada's monetary authority followed a different course. The Bank of Canada gave high priority to holding up the foreign exchange rate of the Canadian dollar. It therefore raised Canadian interest rates in virtual lock-step with American rates, in order to prevent an outflow of funds and attract an inflow instead.

The people who rejoiced in the high exchange rate of the Canadian dollar for European currencies were naive. The lower value of those currencies reflected not some kind of inferiority of Europeans but the superiority of European economic policies. Instead of borrowing at high interest rates, as Canada was doing, European countries were lending at those rates. Instead of shackling their economies by high interest rates that deterred investment, they were stimulating their economies by lower rates that encouraged investment. Instead of piling up indebtedness to foreigners, as we were, they were accumulating foreign assets.

The people who pointed with pride to our dollar's high value in Europe were impressed by a condition produced by an economic policy that European authorities unanimously rejected. Unlike us, they refused to sacrifice basic, long-term interests for the sake of a temporary, superficially impressive advantage that would have heavy future costs.

Canada's resort to high interest rates to strengthen the dollar can be likened to an athlete's resort to anabolic steroids to build up his muscles. Medical opinion differs as to whether steroids enable athletes to improve their actual performance: a good many doctors believe that these drugs only make muscles appear more impressive but do not increase their actual strength. There is no difference of opinion, however, as to the long-run consequences of taking steroids; medical opinion is unanimous that eventual damage is inevitable and severe. In a parallel way it is unclear whether, on balance, the raising of interest rates in Canada to strengthen the dollar was even briefly advantageous. There is no doubt, however, as to the long-term effects; they were unquestionably harmful.

The effect on the price of imports

An increase in Canadian interest rates may indeed attract foreign funds to Canada and thereby prevent – or at least moderate – a fall in the foreign exchange rate of the dollar. It would thereby help against inflation. For if the dollar becomes worth less in foreign currencies, we must pay out more of those dollars when we buy goods from foreigners. Imports, which constitute roughly a quarter of what we buy, cost us about 1 per cent more for each 1-cent drop in the foreign exchange rate of the dollar. A rise in Canadian interest rates that attracts enough foreign funds to prevent a 1-cent drop in the dollar therefore prevents a 1-per-cent increase in the cost of one-quarter of the things we buy.

Between 1966 and 1981 the foreign exchange rate of the dollar fell from 92.8 to 83.4 cents in U.S. funds. That decline of 9.4 cents was responsible for about a 10-per-cent increase in the cost of imports. Our expenditures on imports in 1981 totalled $79 billion; they would have been only $71 billion if the foreign exchange rate of the dollar had still been at its 1966 level. That additional $8 billion paid for imports was about 2 per cent of the total spent in Canada in 1981; because of that 9.4-cent fall in the dollar's foreign exchange rate, the Canadian price level was 2 per cent higher.

The price level was in fact 184 per cent higher overall in 1981 than it had been in 1966. The decline in the foreign exchange rate was responsible for only a tiny fraction of the inflation that occurred over that fifteen-year period. Wage and profit increases were overwhelmingly more important.

Ironically, the increase that occurred in interest rates in Canada caused a bigger rise in the cost of living than did the decline in the dollar's foreign exchange rate. Interest rates soared from the 6- to 8-per-cent level in 1966 to the 20- to 22-per-cent level in 1981, then declined to the 10- to 14-per-cent range in 1985. The aggregate of mortgages outstanding in 1981 was just over $100 billion; the total borrowed from banks and credit unions, for business purposes and personal reasons, was $120 billion. Anyone who took out or renewed a mortgage or loan in 1981 had to pay hugely increased interest charges; the people who took out or renewed mortgages and loans in the next few years were not hit quite so hard, but still had to pay far more than if interest rates had still been at their 1966 level.

It's impossible to compute exactly the additional interest paid by mortgagees and borrowers from banks and credit unions due to the rise in interest rates that occurred between 1966 and the early 1980s. But it certainly would have been at least 4 per cent of $220 billion, putting it in excess of $8 billion, the increase in cost of living caused by the decline in the dollar's foreign exchange rate.

An increase in interest rates to hold down the price of imports amounts to fighting fire with fire. The Bank of Canada caused inflation of the cost of accommodation and the cost of doing business partly in order to prevent inflation in the form of higher prices for imports. Whoever fights fire with fire runs the risk that the fire deliberately caused will do more damage than the fire that would otherwise have occurred. One cannot, of course, be certain of the size of something that never happened because its occurrence was prevented. The possibility certainly exists, however, that the increase in the cost of living in Canada that was caused by the wild rise in interest rates was greater than the increase that would have occurred because of a higher cost of imports.

The policy had other negative consequences. Foreign funds that are attracted to Canada by high interest rates do not come as gifts; they come as loans and investments, on which we will have to pay interest and which we will some day have to repay. If the inflow of that money keeps up the value of the Canadian dollar at the present time, the subsequent outflow of interest and principal repayment will push it down. The value of the dollar will be lower in the future because of our present borrowing; the next generation of Canadians will have to pay more for its imports. We are easing our present inflation problem by a procedure that will aggravate the problem in the future.

Nor is this all. If higher interest rates today do indeed bring a rise in the dollar's foreign exchange rate, severe harm is done to important sectors of the Canadian economy. A higher-priced dollar makes all Canadian goods more expensive to foreigners and therefore makes it more difficult for Canadian exporters to compete in international markets. Where prices on those markets are set in U.S. dollars, as is often the case, a higher exchange rate for the Canadian dollar means lower receipts for Canadian exporters. Thus when wheat sells on the world market for $200 U.S. per tonne, Canadian wheat exporters will get $267 Canadian per tonne when the Canadian dollar stands at 75 cents; if the Canadian dollar is at 85 cents in U.S. funds, wheat exporters will get only $235 Canadian per tonne.

In fairness to the Bank of Canada it must be acknowledged that the interest rate increases it has brought about have been responses to measures instituted in the U.S. The monetary authorities of that country, firmly committed to Friedmanite doctrine, applied increasingly restrictive credit policies that gave rise to a wild escalation of U.S. interest rates. The Bank of Canada feared that if Canadian interest rates did not keep pace with American rates, no foreigners would send their funds to Canada and Canadians would send their funds to the U.S.; the effect would be a sharp reduction of the Canadian dollar's foreign exchange rate. In order to prevent such a decline, the Bank matched the increases in U.S. interest rates applied by that country's monetary authorities; in effect, Canada's monetary policy was made in Washington. Partly as a result of having credit policies that were in lock-step with those of the U.S., Canada experienced the sharp recession of 1981–82, together with the other adverse effects produced by high interest rates.

TWELVE

The Lowering of Standards

We make our fortunes and we call them fate.
DISRAELI

During the past two decades, dramatic advances have been achieved in a number of sciences. Physicists have built vehicles capable of voyaging to the moon and exploring the universe; chemists have developed drugs that heal illness and give relief from pain; botanists have bred new plant varieties that yield far bigger crops.

There is one major field, however, in which regression, not advance, has occurred since the 1960s: economics. The economies of many industrialized countries, of all Western countries, are performing less well than they did in the 1950s and 1960s. Inflation and unemployment, the two most severe economic afflictions, are everywhere more serious than they were in those decades.

This deterioration in economic performance has not been attributable to negligence on the part of economists nor to lack of effort on their part. Enormous numbers of economic studies have been carried out; innumerable explanatory hypotheses have been developed; striking advances have been achieved in methodology; analytical techniques have become far more sophisticated. Nevertheless, despite the immense range and scale of economic study that has been carried out, the performance of actual economic systems is worse than it used to be.

Cynics might be pardoned for suggesting that the inverse relationship between theoretical expertise and actual economic performance has not been pure happenstance. Contemporary economic study has sought primarily to establish mathematical relationships between precisely measured variables. But the most important factor in economic activity – the human factor – cannot be measured exactly. It has therefore been largely ignored: the unmeasurable has been the unmentionable. The regression of Western economies may be attributable, at least in part, to economic study that has diverted attention away from the most important determinant of economic performance.

The current inferior performance of the Canadian economy is not dismissed as a temporary aberration caused by some chance development; instead it is declared to be the new norm. Economists warn that we should not expect to have again the combination of 2 or 3 per cent inflation and 3 or 4 per cent unemployment that existed throughout most of the 1950s and 1960s. And we certainly cannot expect to have the virtually zero unemployment and zero inflation that existed during World War II.

As a matter of fact, sophisticated economic doctrine now declares it to be absolutely necessary to have an unemployment rate of at least 7 or 8 per cent – that is, the number of unemployed in Canada must never be less than 1 million. A decline below this level will precipitate dangerous aggravation of the inflation problem. Gerald Bouey attributed what he called the "great inflation" of the 1970s to excessively stimulative policies applied by governments. The unemployment rate averaged over 7 per cent in Canada during the 1970s; in his opinion, evidently, the government should have applied policies that would have generated a rate of unemployment *higher* than 7 per cent.

In effect, unemployed Canadians are to be the country's shock troops in the battle against inflation. It's hardly caricature to suggest that unemployed persons might be given a badge on which is inscribed the proud word "UNEMPLOYED," identifying them as members of the gallant army that is protecting the country from inflation.

To maintain that army at the necessary strength, the government is urged to apply sufficiently restrictive economic policies so that at least a million Canadians will always be without jobs. Whether they liked it or not, unemployment would be imposed on them. A believer in freedom of choice would suggest that as an alternative way of recruiting the necessary million-strong army of unemployed, the government might invite people to volunteer, appealing to old-fashioned patriotism or offering some kind of inducement not to work. It could shame them into not working. In England during World War I patriotic ladies standing at intersections handed white feathers to sturdy young men who passed by wearing civilian clothes.

If there weren't enough unemployed in Canada, the government could recruit ladies to hand white feathers to persons about to enter their places of employment.

Something like this has actually been happening in Canada. Unemployed men and women have staged angry demonstrations, demanding work. The people who demonstrated in this way have been condemned for making unreasonable, intemperate demands. They have been accused of selfishly refusing to recognize that their joblessness is vitally needed to hold down inflation.

The term "welfare bum" was coined years ago to apply to individuals who lived off public welfare financed by the rest of the community. Unemployed people who today demand jobs could be called "work bums"; they are demanding employment for themselves that would burden the rest of the community.

A strategy of economic restraint that reduces the quantity and quality of job opportunity is totally incompatible with the expectations of young people graduating from our educational system.

Schools don't just impart knowledge; they influence attitudes and expectations as well. The young people who attend Canada's high schools become conditioned to expect that when they graduate they will get interesting, well-paid jobs. University students acquire expectations pitched several notches higher. Everybody's expectations are amplified by modern advertising and the portrayal of sophisticated lifestyles in movies and on television.

Ottawa's policies of restraint, by limiting the amount and quality of employment opportunity, have generated intense frustration for a great many of Canada's younger people. Hundreds of thousands of high school and university graduates have been unable to get jobs or have found only jobs far below their capabilities. The Canadian economy has been seriously out of joint with the Canadian educational system.

The young graduates have not got the jobs and the country has not had the benefit of the contributions that bright, educated minds could have made – the new products they could have devised, the new techniques for dealing with pollution, the new ways of conserving and producing energy, the new ways of dealing with social problems. We have not enjoyed the artistic contributions they could have made. Instead, we have watched many of them staging angry demonstrations, flaunting and breaking the laws of a society that appears indifferent to their needs, suffering deterioration in personality and spirit.

The clock of education cannot be turned back. Tomorrow's young Canadians will insist on educational opportunities at least as good as those provided to yesterday's and today's young Canadians. Our schools will continue to turn out large numbers of people seeking appropriate employment.

Continuation of restraint policies will maintain the disparity between the qualifications of graduates and the job opportunities available to them. The number of well-educated, frustrated people will increase; we can expect the "youth" problem to grow in size and increase in degree.

During the past few years financial retrenchment has caused an appreciable reduction in the quality of some public services, with damaging consequences for the populations served. Provincial governments have allotted less money to highway maintenance; road journeys are therefore more arduous and accidents and vehicle damage more likely. A number of municipal authorities have reduced the size of their fire departments and police forces; their communities are now less well protected against fire and crime. Public libraries are open fewer hours per week. In some cities arrangements for garbage and sewage disposal have not kept pace with population growth; disagreeable sights and smells are therefore more common and hazards to health more severe. These curtailments are expected to continue indefinitely. More services may be subject to retrenchment: a federal cabinet minister warned in 1986 that home delivery of mail may soon be limited to alternate days – or ended altogether.

We face the prospect of deterioration in another important aspect of economic performance. A cardinal measure of any society is the way it looks after weaker members who can't fully provide for themselves. Between 1940 and 1970 Canada introduced measures to help large categories of persons who had economic difficulty: people who had lost their jobs; older persons who could no longer work and had little or no savings, little or no pension income; parents whose low incomes made it difficult for them to provide adequately for their children; people who required costly medical treatment. To hold down administrative costs and avoid the need for "means tests," allowances were paid to all persons in the age categories where the proportion of needy persons was very large – with the consequence that aid was given to a significant number of persons who didn't need it. Medical treatment was provided without charge to everyone in those categories, including those persons who were quite able to pay the cost themselves.

The federal government provided most of the funds for these programs. It paid the allowances to older persons and families with children, supplemented the insurance fund out of which payments were made to persons who had become unemployed, gave grants to provincial governments towards the cost of medical services. As well, the federal government began to make contributions towards the cost of university education; till the 1950s this cost had been borne entirely by provincial governments. In making its grants to provincial governments, Ottawa applied the principle of "equalization"; that is, it employed formulas under which relatively more money was given to the administrations of the poorer provinces, to enable them to provide public services that would be on a par with those provided in the richer provinces.

The Conservative government elected in 1984 set out to hold down the federal government's outlay on all these programs as part of a strategy to cut down the government's overall spending and thereby reduce its budget deficit. It raised the contributions to the unemployment insurance fund required from employers and workers, partially "de-indexed" family allowances (decreed that they would be increased to compensate for inflation only by the inflation rate *minus* 3 per cent), and reduced the growth rate of federal grants to provincial governments below the level proposed by the previous federal administration. In addition the new federal administration proposed de-indexing old age pensions, but it withdrew the proposal because of the furious opposition that it encountered. The effect of these measures is to reduce the amount of assistance given to poorer Canadians; the Canadian economy, according to the criterion of how generously it provides for the community's poorer members, will perform less well in the future than it has done in the past.

Deterioration has occurred – and full recovery appears unlikely – in another aspect of economic performance. The sharp rise in interest rates that occurred in the 1970s and early 1980s enhanced the advantage of inherited wealth, increased the handicap of those who received no inheritance. Poor borrowers had to pay more to

rich lenders for the same financial service, widening income in-
equality. Interest rates have come down from the peak they reached
in 1981 but are still well above the levels of the 1950s and 1960s
and appear likely to remain so. The burden that high interest rates
impose on the poor and the bonus they confer on the wealthy will
continue.

The Conservative administration that came to power in 1984 en-
thusiastically took up the suggestion, put forward by the Macdonald
royal commission, that Canada should seek free trade with the United
States. The proposal was based on the economic principle that every
nation would achieve maximum productivity and income by con-
centrating on the production of the goods it is best qualified to make,
and selling some of these products to other countries in exchange
for goods that *they* are best qualified to produce. Trade barriers
interfere with this beneficial international specialization, harming
not only the countries against which they are directed but also the
countries that maintain them. Countries that reduce or eliminate
their trade barriers against one another would all benefit. They would
lose inefficient industries that need protection against imports, but
would achieve expansion of efficient industries that would have free
access to an additional market. The jobs gained would be more productive than the jobs lost.

Economic theory does not speak to the *number* of jobs lost and
gained by the removal of trade barriers; it only declares that the
same workers will be more productive in a regime of free trade than
they will be in a regime of trade barriers. Their number could be
smaller, in both the short run and the long run. In the short run
there may be a net loss of jobs in the country because the industries
harmed by the reduction of barriers to imports contract quickly,
while the industries that are helped, expand slowly. But even when
these industries do expand, the number of additional workers they
hire may be small; they may increase their productive capacity primarily by installing more, bigger, and better equipment. Productivity per worker may indeed increase in the country, but fewer workers
may have jobs.

If the commonly made forecasts are correct, then, for years to come,
we will have substantially higher unemployment rates than we had

between 1940 and 1970. There will continue to be enormous waste, in the form of failure to produce a huge amount of goods and services for which we have the productive capability; there will be widespread hurt in the form of bitterness and frustration felt by persons who would like to work but can't get a job. In addition there will be regressive redistribution of the national income that favours the already well-to-do and burdens the economically weak.

In his novel *1984*, George Orwell described Newspeak, a language with cryptic grammatical forms and phrases in which the ordinary meaning of words is cynically distorted. "Big Brother" is an omnipresent watchful eye that sees absolutely everything and notes for punishment every deviation from rules laid down by a tyrannical authority. The government department with the responsibility of waging war is the Ministry of Peace; the department that spreads propaganda is the Ministry of Truth; a forced-labour camp is a joycamp.

Much of today's economic reporting and forecasting is in Newspeak. Commentators glowingly declared in 1984 that the Canadian economy had recovered from the 1981–82 recession, although the unemployment rate was still in double digits, not too far below the levels of the 1930s when Canada experienced the worse depression in history. What's more, the persistence of such rates of unemployment in the future will apparently not prevent Canada from being regarded as prosperous.

The authors of this judgment employ only a single criterion in their assessment of national economic performance: how much is produced. If national output increases by 2 per cent a year, the country is declared to be prosperous, no matter how high the unemployment rate, no matter how unequally the national income is being distributed.

But in any sane assessment of national economic performance, the unemployment rate would be the primary and governing consideration. A low unemployment rate would indicate good economic performance, in that the country was effectively using its potential. A high unemployment rate would unambiguously denote inferior performance: the country would be suffering waste in the form of failure to produce worthwhile goods for which it had the capacity.

The waste of unproduced output is not the greatest harm caused by unemployment. Most people who are unemployed suffer frustration from the denial of opportunity to fulfil themselves through work. They live a succession of formless days that lack the pattern of regular employment; they have only the limited purchasing power of savings, insurance, or welfare.

No economy, no matter how much it produces, can be considered to be operating acceptably, to be "recovered" or "prosperous," if one worker in ten suffers the trauma of unemployment. And the psychological damage extends beyond those who are jobless. A high rate of unemployment causes apprehension among people who still have jobs. Their lives are darkened by the fear that they might also become unemployed. They don't buy things they would like to have for fear that they might lose their jobs and would then badly need the money they had spent. They don't quit a job they dislike out of fear that they might not get another one.

Canada produced in the early 1980s considerably more than it did in the 1950s, both in aggregate terms and per capita. Thanks to additions to the national stock of machinery and equipment, improvements in education and training, the acquisition of experience, the discovery of additional resource deposits, our productive capacity was far greater than it had been thirty years earlier. By any sensible standard we were, however, more prosperous in the 1950s than we have been so far in the 1980s. The unemployment rate then averaged just over 4 per cent; there was an amplitude of goods and, even more important, an amplitude of jobs. The general mood was one of confidence and well-being. There wasn't the waste, the frustration, the apprehension generated by large-scale unemployment.

The phrase "wartime prosperity" reflects the overwhelming importance of adequate job opportunities as a criterion of economic performance. Because a great many civilian goods were in short supply or not available at all, the material well-being of the Canadian population was probably at a lower level than it had been in peacetime. But everyone who wanted to work could get a job. So times were good; the country was reckoned to be dazzlingly prosperous.

The declaration by some commentators that Canada will be prosperous even though the unemployment rate is 10 to 12 per cent corresponds to a doctor's assuring a patient that his health is excellent, subject only to the minor qualification that he has a terminal cancer. Were George Orwell alive today, he might have included some contemporary economic statements as forms of Newspeak. A revised definition of "prosperity" now makes it possible to label an economy prosperous despite its gross failure in respect to what has hitherto been considered to be the most critical aspect of its performance.

THIRTEEN

There Are Better Options

Good reasons must, of force, give place to better.
    SHAKESPEARE, Julius Caesar

An effectively performing Canadian economy would be one in which the evils of unemployment and inflation were minimal, income was fairly distributed, reasonable progress was being achieved. The country would be utilizing fully its productive power, producing as many useful goods and services as it was physically capable of doing. There would be little or none of the inflation that reduces buying power and has generally unsettling effects. The distribution of income among individuals would reward those who applied superior efforts and skills and undertook greater risks and responsibilities. At the same time, a decent income would be provided to those who were unable to provide for themselves. The technology employed would be constantly improving. The rest of the industrialized world is likely to continue achieving technological progress; we would want Canada to at least keep up and not become an economic backwater.

The federal government – with its absolute authority over all Canadians, its unlimited power of taxation, its right to create the country's lawful currency – is the agency that should regulate the Canadian economy to ensure that it performs properly. It alone has all the necessary powers.

To generate jobs in the country whenever the number was insufficient, the government would have to bring about an increase in overall spending. By reducing the personal income tax, it could procure an increase in spending by the general public on consumer goods; by reducing the corporate income tax, it would leave businesses more funds that they could invest and, as well, induce them to undertake more investment by making the return on it more profitable. The government could give subsidies to businesses to induce them to expand their operations and take on more employees. The central bank could liberalize credit and reduce interest rates to make investment easier and more attractive. The government could give loans or grants to foreigners to enable them to buy more of our exports. The government could spend more itself, on public works and public services, and give grants to provincial and municipal administrations to enable them to spend more on their public works and public services. Employment would be created in the construction and improvement of docks, highways, water supply and sewage disposal systems, in the extension of research, in the improvement of education and training.

The money spent by the government to generate additional jobs should be obtained by borrowing and not by taxation. For if the money were obtained by taxation, there could be severe negative effects. Persons and firms that had to pay higher taxes would reduce their spending, causing lay-offs in the establishments that experienced declines in sales. The number of jobs lost could be equal to the number created by the government's new programs. The total number of jobs might increase little or not at all; the main effect would be to cause different people to be unemployed. The country's overall well-being might even be reduced: that would be the case if the newly created jobs contributed less to the country than the ones that were eliminated by the increase in taxation.

The borrowing to finance a program of job generation should be done entirely within Canada and entirely by the federal government. If all borrowing were done within Canada, no burden would be created for the Canadian people: all interest payments and principal repayments would be made to them; no money would leave the country. What's more, we would not experience the negative effects on employment that are caused by inflows of foreign funds that raise the foreign exchange rate of the Canadian dollar. Our exports would not be made more expensive to foreigners, nor would imports be made cheaper for Canadians, as happens when the dollar's foreign exchange rate rises. And Canada would not be subjected to the danger of being unable to pay its foreign debts – as could happen if we were unable to earn through exports all the foreign exchange needed to pay debts owed to foreigners. We would avoid as well the danger that a drop in the dollar's foreign exchange rate would increase the burden of a debt owed outside the country. Any Canadian agency that took out a ten-year $100-million loan on Wall Street in 1975 had to pay $140 million for the $100 million U.S. that it paid back in 1985. That sort of unexpected blow does not occur when money is borrowed in Canada.

And if the federal government did all the borrowing, in Canada, the financial load would be distributed in the optimum way; it would be borne by the appropriate agency. For the federal government is the main financial beneficiary of the public revenue that is generated when unemployed people get jobs; it collects more personal income tax, more corporate income tax, more sales tax; it pays out less in unemployment insurance. Provincial governments also collect additional tax when unemployed residents get jobs, but the financial benefit that accrues to the federal government is far greater: its tax rates are much higher, and it alone gains the very important benefit of a saving in unemployment insurance payments. Finally, the federal government can never be unable to pay Canadian creditors: it alone has unlimited power of taxation over them and the authority to create, in whatever quantity it decides, the kind of money that it is obligated to pay them.

While the federal government should do all the borrowing to finance job generation, the actual projects should not be federal ones only. A large part of the money raised should be handed over to municipal and provincial governments, to be spent on public works and public services for which they are responsible. Federal politicians ought not to take the view that the money is "theirs," to be used only as they see fit, simply because they are in the best position to raise and spend it. That money belongs to the people of Canada and should be used for whatever projects would best serve their needs. It would be wrong for the federal government to generate jobs purely in areas of its own jurisdiction – enlarging the armed forces, expanding rail networks, building new docks – while provincial highways badly needed reconstruction and cities needed better water supplies and sewage disposal systems.

The Canadian historical record includes the following account:

> Over the past four years, total government expenditure (including provincial and municipal) has increased from about $1 billion a year to about $5 billions a year. At the same time, unemployment has virtually disappeared and the gross value of Canada's output of goods and services has increased from $5 billions a year to more than $9 billions. Even after allowing for an over-all price increase of, say, 20 per cent, the figures indicate that the volume of output has shown a

tremendous expansion, which has not yet ceased. . . . The
experience of the last four years has shown that Government
war expenditure on a sufficient scale can produce full
employment.

These are not the words of a woolly radical, ignorant and reckless
of fiscal realities. They were written by Graham Towers, the first
governor of the Bank of Canada, previously the assistant general
manager of the Royal Bank of Canada. He made these observations
in his report to the minister of finance for the year 1942.

The figures he cited were astronomical in his day. The Canadian
economy was then much smaller than it is now, and the value of a
dollar was much greater. The equivalent increase in government
spending today would be from $50 billion to $250 billion.

It was this immense increase in government spending, financed
entirely by taxation and borrowing within Canada, that paid for the
country's war effort. That effort, including enlistments in the armed
forces and jobs in war industry, totally liquidated the 10- to 15-per-
cent unemployment that existed when the war began. The politicians
and business leaders who today vehemently declare that government
spending can't solve the unemployment problem speak from conviction that is untarnished by knowledge of the factual record. They
get their proof from one another's speeches, not from the facts.

We need small projects as well as big ones. Our authorities should
stop depending for jobs on gigantic, high-profile developments that
may or may not occur – the discovery of new oil fields or mineral
deposits, a decision by Japan to buy huge quantities of our coal. If
such lucky breaks occur, we should certainly take advantage of them,
but we should not lamely accept high rates of unemployment while
we wait and hope for them.

There is a moral for Canada in Aesop's fable about the man
who owned an orchard and had three lazy sons who refused to do
the tedious work of pruning, hoeing, and cultivating. When the man
became very old and knew that death was approaching, he called the
sons together and revealed a secret to them. Many years before, he
said, he had buried a pot filled with gold coins under one of the trees
in the orchard, but he could not tell them exactly where it was.
After the old man's death the three sons feverishly searched the

orchard. But although they dug up the soil around every tree, going well below the surface, they found no pot of gold. Bitterly they concluded that their father's story had been fanciful; they should have known better than to take seriously an improbable claim made by an old man on the brink of death.

That autumn, thanks to the thorough cultivation of its soil, the orchard yielded a huge harvest, a far greater one than it had ever yielded when the old man had done all the work himself. The sons sold the crop for a very large amount of money, as much as they had thought they would come upon in the pot of gold. They then realized the trick their father had played on them, and ever afterwards they thoroughly cultivated the soil in the orchard.

The Canadian scene has provided a contemporary parallel to this ancient tale. Federal economic policy has depended for jobs on happenstance – the discovery of oil pools and mineral deposits, favourable decisions by foreign governments. But there is plenty of worthwhile, if unspectacular, work that we could arrange without waiting for lucky breaks. Stimulative policy applied by the federal government could generate jobs that would increase our output of food, clothing, and housing, that would make our highways safer, our parks pleasanter. The work done could contribute as much to national well-being as some spectacular long shot – a long shot that might never occur.

There is another way, besides job creation, for the government to reduce unemployment. It could arrange that the available amount of work be divided up more evenly: instead of nine people working full-time and one person being idle full-time, all ten could work but with each one working nine-tenths of full time. Work-time per person could be reduced in a number of ways: hours worked per day could be reduced, days worked per week, weeks worked per year, years worked per lifetime.

One reason why European countries have lower unemployment rates than Canada is that their workers have longer vacations. In Sweden workers now get a minimum of six weeks of vacation per year; in France and Germany they get a minimum of four weeks. In Canada the minimum designated by law is two weeks, and that's all that many workers get.

What the Swedes, French, and Germans do, we could do, too.

There would be widespread benefit if the standard working year in Canada were reduced to forty-eight weeks; a good many people now unemployed would get jobs; a good many people now working would enjoy longer vacations; there would be additional jobs in the industries that cater to vacationers. Since the total amount of time worked in the country would be no less than before, there would be no reduction in national output. The government could compensate employers for any costs involved, using funds that would otherwise be paid out as unemployment insurance to jobless workers.

Special programs might be instituted for particular categories of person. Sixty-year-old men who had done heavy physical labour all their lives might be permitted to retire at full pension – or perhaps to work part-time till their retirement with no reduction in pay. Women with small children at home might be given time off, without loss of pay, so that they could spend more time with their children – and someone else could have work. The cost of such programs, too, could be covered with money that would have been paid out in unemployment insurance.

The government is now operating a work-sharing program under which firms whose business has shrunk can reduce the work week, typically to three or four days, instead of laying anyone off. Employees are able to claim unemployment insurance benefits for the one or two days they are not working. The scheme could be extended: the government could offer financial inducement to firms whose business was at normal levels to reduce the number of days worked by employees each week and therefore hire more people. A few test projects would certainly be worth trying, in which businesses are induced to give their workers time off, filling in with people who would otherwise have been unemployed, and the government covering whatever cost is involved.

Stimulative policies must be selected with care, of course. Judgment would have to be exercised to choose the most appropriate combination of measures for whatever unemployment problem develops. Each type of measure has its advantages and drawbacks; each suits a particular set of circumstances best. Thus if the country's most pressing need were for improvement in the living standard of its people, a policy of economic stimulation would emphasize reduction of the personal income tax that would increase the public's ability to buy consumer goods. If the country's greatest need were for additional industrial plant, emphasis would be on reduction of the corporate income tax, to enable and induce increase in investment. If the country's greatest need were for improvement of its public facilities and public services, then emphasis would be on government spending to achieve these improvements.

There are other issues to be taken into account. Tax reductions might not always be effective: people whose taxes were reduced might just save the additional money – or spend it on imported goods or on trips outside of Canada. Businesses that paid less tax might not invest the extra funds: they might simply add to their reserves or pay larger dividends to shareholders. Subsidies given to businesses might not induce them to spend any more of their own money. The consequences could be only a small increase – or none at all – in private-sector spending and employment. On the other hand, if the government decided to increase its spending on public works and public services, the effects would be certain and immediate. The authorities would have to judge which type of stimulative measure was most appropriate at any particular time, taking into account the possibility that tax reductions might not generate the desired increase in employment or do so only after a long delay, while increased public spending would bring certain and immediate results.

Finally, it would not be necessary for the government to attempt to create jobs for *all* the people who were unemployed; the government could assume that if it created some jobs, in either the public sector or the private sector, then additional jobs would be generated indirectly. The people who got jobs as a direct result of the government's initiative would increase their spending; so would firms that enjoyed increase in their sales. As a consequence, more jobs would come into being in a host of other industries; the number of jobs thereby created could be large. In considering the scale of a stimulative program, therefore, the government should take into account the number of jobs that would likely come into being through spin-off effect.

Expenditure increases and tax reductions applied by the government should be sufficient – but no more than sufficient; application of these measures in excess will cause inflation. They will be non-inflationary so long as they serve to put unemployed people to work, with their pay corresponding to their productivity; the increase in national spending will be accompanied by an offsetting increase in national output. But if the total of private- and public-sector spending rises by more than the amount needed to generate jobs for all the country's unemployed, inflation must result: more money will be chasing the same amount of goods. Inflation may in fact result even if the amount of additional spending is not excessive. This will be the outcome if the work done by newly employed people is absolutely useless, contributing nothing to national output; if they are paid at rates in excess of their productivity; if some of the extra spending is used not to hire unemployed people, but to fatten the paycheques of people already working and widen the profit margins of firms already in business.

As ample experience indicates, we may suffer inflation even if the government is not applying programs intended to generate productive jobs for all the country's unemployed. Union leaders, in negotiating new contracts, may demand wage increases that are in excess of productivity gains, threatening to call a strike if their demands are not met. Employers, to avoid the harm and loss they would suffer if their employees went on strike, may grant wage increases that raise production costs and therefore require increases in selling prices.

That this should happen is virtually inevitable. At all times there are bound to be some unions that have great bargaining power because their members perform critically important services, and they are sure to apply that power to the full in order to extract the highest possible pay increases. A large increase won by a high-profile union produces a snowball effect. Other unions adopt it as a target, and other employers feel an obligation to conform. Every employer, what's more, can feel easier about raising prices when other firms are paying their employees at higher rates: each firm's customers – who are employees of other firms – will have received pay increases that enable them to pay higher prices.

During periods of economic recession, on the other hand, when there is a great deal of unemployment, unions accept contracts that provide for only small wage increases, no increases, or actual reductions. With the average increase in pay close to the increase in national output, the inflation rate tumbles – as it did in the recession that began in 1982, when the unemployment rate was at double-digit levels. However, a low rate of inflation that is generated by recession is unlikely to continue indefinitely. Improvement in the economy, notably a decline in the unemployment rate, restores labour's bargaining power, and labour leaders apply that renewed power to extract wage increases that are well above productivity growth. The cycle of large wage increases raising production costs, making necessary large price increases that justify further large wage increases, is resumed. The economy is likely to operate in stop-and-go fashion, alternating between high rates of unemployment combined with low rates of inflation during periods of recession, and low rates of unemployment combined with high rates of inflation during periods of prosperity.

The prevention of inflation indispensably requires that the national increase in income correspond to the increase in national output – that if Canada produces only 2 per cent more, then the total of wages and profits increase by only 2 per cent. If wages and profits increase by more than 2 per cent, inflation is inevitable; the arithmetic is implacable.

There are three broad procedures for preventing exercises of market power that result in inflationary increase in the national total of wages and profits: intimidation – the threat of some kind of punishment; coercion – limitation imposed by public authority on the exercise of private powers; and consensus – agreement among those who possess power to refrain from using it in mutually harmful ways. So far we have relied primarily on intimidation, on measures that generated the frightening spectre of unemployment for those who insisted on large pay increases. It has proven to be quite effective – but only once the spectre was sufficiently large and menacing. Obviously, however, if we rely on unemployment to curb inflation, then we cannot have both price stability and full employment. If we are to have both, we must use one of the other anti-inflation strategies – coercion and consensus – or some combination of them.

If we are to have both full employment and price stability, we must use some means other than the brutal club of unemployment to prevent increases in wages and profits that are in excess of increase in national output. The federal government has, in fact, applied three different strategies to prevent or at least limit inflationary increases in wages and profit margins: "freezes," "voluntary guidelines," and "controls."

During World War II Ottawa "froze" wages and prices by forbidding any increases, and it taxed away profits in excess of amounts previously earned. In 1969–70 the Prices and Incomes Commission laid down "guidelines" for wages and profits, appealing to labour and management to voluntarily limit their wage increases and profit margins to the guideline figures. From 1975 to 1978 the Anti-Inflation Board controlled wages and profit margins, permitting only such increases as it considered to be justifiable. (Similar boards in other countries simply forbade any increase above a designated figure; thus a British board in the 1960s decreed that no employee was to receive a pay increase in excess of £6 a week.)

Each of these strategies for holding down wage and profit increases has severe shortcomings. Freezes and controls have been furiously opposed by labour, cordially disliked by businesspeople, deeply deplored by economists. Labour leaders, committed to the principle that wages should be set through negotiation between an employer and representatives of the employees, absolutely oppose the dictation of wages by a government body. Union officials have a deeply personal interest here: the most dramatic and significant task they typically perform is that of negotiating new contracts. If wages were simply decreed by a public authority, their leadership role would be substantially eroded.

Businesses object to controls over their profits that prevent them from capitalizing on juicy opportunities – especially since the government gives no undertaking to assist them when conditions change and they lose money. As well, they are irritated by the close surveillance to which they are subject when a freeze or control is imposed, the unending reports they must send in. Economists deplore freezes and controls because they prevent markets from operating efficiently. In their view, a price rise that occurs because a product is in short supply or strong demand serves useful purposes: it induces production of larger amounts; it removes from the market those people who don't strongly need or want the good. Prevention of such a price increase deters the production of desirable additional output and makes it possible for the entire available supply to be acquired by people to whom it isn't very important – while people who want it badly aren't able to get any.

In any case, controls are all too easy to evade. Black markets are likely to develop, where buyers secretly pay sellers more than the legal prices. Some producers circumvent the controls by reducing the quality or quantity of the product that they sell at the controlled price. Some employers secretly give workers more than the regulations allow. If all controls were to be effectively enforced, half the country would have to be watching the other half. Realistically, the authorities have to rely on voluntary compliance, so it's only in wartime, when people are imbued with patriotic fervour, that compliance would be general. In peacetime, very large numbers of people would have few fears or qualms about violating price and wage control regulations.

Voluntary guidelines have been contemptuously dismissed by labour leaders since they, too, would replace negotiation as the wage-setting procedure. What's more, since compliance would be entirely voluntary, the restraint exercised by one party might not be matched by others. Labour leaders predict that if workers were to agree to small wage increases or none as their contribution to fighting inflation, businesses would still charge as much as the market would bear; the self-denial of workers would merely mean larger profits for their employers.

Other strategies are available and are being applied effectively in other countries. Admittedly, those countries have not achieved the golden ideal of full employment combined with absolute price stability, but their economic performance has been decidedly better than Canada's.

One possible strategy is profit-sharing, which is widely practised in Japan. If workers are given a share of profit instead of an increase in their hourly wage, the effect is anti-inflationary, for two significant reasons. No increase occurs in production cost. Whatever increase workers receive in their pay comes out of the firm's productivity: the increases in money payments made to them are matched by increases in the firm's net output. Secondly, profit-sharing helps keep prices down insofar as it brings about increase in productivity. Every increase in the quantity of goods produced in the country exercises downward pressure on prices by increasing market supplies. Profit-sharing is likely to foster more diligent effort by workers and consequently an increase in the total of goods produced.

It's very likely that we will be able to elicit workers' best efforts only if we adopt some form of profit-sharing. For workers today are very different from those of the past. The ordinary Canadian worker years ago was a humble person who had little education, expected only a modest income, accepted without question the right of an élite to have an income far above his own. The commonly used legal phrase "master and servant" epitomized his status. He did his best on the job out of a spirit of craftsmanship, out of a sense of feudal obligation to his employer, out of fear of being fired and replaced by someone else who would do the job better.

Things are very different today. Workers do not regard themselves as the servants of others. Practically all have completed high school. They are bombarded with advertising that seductively displays a lavish array of desirable goods and proclaims their entitlement to a goodly share. They drive cars and are therefore accustomed to the sense of power that comes from having hundreds of horsepower surge in response to the touch of a toe. They are likely to be members of unions whose officers bargain aggressively for the highest rates of pay that can be extracted from employers; in concert with fellow-workers, they are prepared to go on strike if an employer refuses to accede to their union's demands.

If today's workers are to be induced to do their best, they must be given incentives that did not have to be given to workers in the past. Profit-sharing is such an incentive. If they were promised a share in the company's profits, they would have a material reason for performing as well as they could. That individual incentive would be reinforced by the pressure of their peers, for each worker's failure to do his or her best would mean loss of income for the others. If ownership-sharing were practised as well, workers would have a completely different attitude towards employers. The company would now be "their" firm. The boss would be not their opposition but their quarterback; effort and ingenuity previously devoted to frustrating the boss would be applied instead to helping him or her.

Profit-sharing could be introduced quite easily and in very short order. New wage contracts could be signed for only small increases in hourly pay – perhaps even no increases – but with employees receiving a designated share of their employer's profit. In negotiating new contracts, union representatives would bargain not so much for increases in hourly rates, but rather for increases in the percentage of the profit to be given to employees. If they bargained shrewdly, the workers they represented would get more pay than if new contracts had provided only for increases in hourly rates. U.S. autoworkers did very well in 1984, thanks to contract provisions that entitled them to a share of car-makers' huge profits that year.

If the government believed that a wide extension of profit-sharing would be good for the country, it need not rely merely on hope and prayer. It could actively promote it by offering tax concessions to the two parties concerned – to workers who agreed to accept only small increases in their hourly rates, to firms that agreed to share profits with employees. The cost to the government would be amply justified by the resultant reduction in inflation and the improved social climate. In any case, that cost could be slight or nil as improvements in productivity generated increased tax revenues. One of the major reasons for Japan's economic success is that its firms share profits with employees. Extension of profit-sharing in Canada would be a major step towards the achievement of the labour–management relationships that are critically necessary in a country whose labour force is well educated, well informed, and well organized.

Another strategy against cost-push inflation would be to allow labour and management to negotiate wage contracts as they saw fit, but require that the average pay increase be no greater than the increase in national output. This requirement could be achieved through a consensus of all the participants in wage negotiations, or it could be imposed by government decree. This type of strategy has been applied in Sweden for years. A committee representing all blue-collar unions meets each year with a committee representing all the employers, and the two negotiate the pay for the next year of every category of worker represented. Prior to the negotiations the two committees are told what percentage increase in Sweden's national output is expected in the coming year, and they are cautioned that while the wage of any particular category of worker could be increased to any degree, the average increase in wages for all workers must not exceed the rate of increase in national output.

While in principle this procedure should have absolutely prevented inflation, in fact Sweden has had inflation rates comparable to Canada's. The primary reason has been that local unions that have considerable bargaining power have insisted on higher rates of pay than those negotiated by national committees. Sweden has had very low rates of unemployment, however, and its overall economic performance has been markedly superior to that of most industrialized countries. While the mode of wage-setting has not prevented inflation, it has kept it in check and thereby enabled the government to apply the strongly stimulative policies that keep the unemployment rate very low.

There would be no inflation if a broad consensus could exist that all wage increases should be in the near neighbourhood of the country's growth rate, so that no one demands significantly more. Such a consensus did exist in Canada from 1950 to 1966, when there was general agreement that a 4-per-cent pay increase was reasonable, that only workers with superior claims deserved as much as 5 or 6 per cent, and that increases of 2 or 3 per cent were only slightly below the average and would have to be accepted by workers whose bargaining power was inferior.

Another way of controlling the aggregate of pay increases, so far not attempted anywhere, would be to require that all wage contracts be for one year and that they be negotiated at the same time, as is done in Sweden. But each labour–management group would carry on quite independently, being free to negotiate any size of wage increase. Once all the negotiations had been concluded, the average of all the increases would be calculated. If this average turned out to be higher than the prospective increase in national output, the government would decree that all the increases that had been negotiated would have to be scaled down before they were implemented, so as to bring their average to conformity with the expected increase in national output. For example, if the average of the increases agreed to in the negotiations had been 12 per cent, but national output was expected to increase by only 3 per cent, every increase would have to be reduced to one-quarter the figure that had been negotiated.

Such a procedure would prevent inflation since it would ensure that the total of increases in pay conformed to the increase in the country's actual output. And it would prevent inflation in a way that did not involve government intervention in the marketplace. The original ratios of the wage increases of different labour categories, produced by market forces, would be preserved. A union that had won a 20-per-cent increase would still get twice the increase of a union that had won only a 10-per-cent increase at the bargaining table, but it would get 5 per cent while the other union got 2.5 per cent. The amount of actual purchasing power gained by workers as a result of a wage raise would not be affected by the application of this anti-inflation procedure. Instead of receiving a large increase in pay that brought only a small increase in purchasing power because of inflation, a worker would get a small increase in pay but in a regime of stable prices. The increase in actual purchasing power could be exactly the same.

Another governmental measure to prevent inflationary increase in rates of pay could be to give income tax reductions to workers who agreed to small increases in their wage rates. If rates of pay rose very little, there would be no cause for increase in prices. Workers, meanwhile, need not lose anything because of their forbearance; the reduction in income tax payable could constitute full compensation.

There is one procedural change in the handling of the federal government's finances that would be well worth making. Instead of paying interest to the holders of its bonds, the government should give them tax credits. In 1985 Ottawa collected $42 billion from individual Canadians through its income tax on individuals, $12 billion from Canadian businesses through its tax on their profits, and $19 billion in sales tax, excise taxes, and duties on imports. Meanwhile, in the same year, it paid $22 billion in interest to the Canadian individuals, businesses, and other organizations that had bought its bonds. Therefore, collecting a total of $73 billion in tax and paying back $22 billion in bond interest, it took $51 billion from the private sector. The same effect could have been achieved if the government had given bond-holders tax credits equal to the amount of interest it owed them. Its actual tax collection would then have been only $51 billion, the amount it needed for purposes other than making interest payments to Canadian bond-holders.

Probably the federal tax liability of some bond-owners would have been less than the amount the government owed them as interest. If the tax credits were transferable, such bond-holders would have been able to sell their surplus credits to taxpayers who could have used them. The final effect would still have been that the government collected only $51 billion in tax from persons and firms and paid no interest to Canadian bond-holders.

This procedure would eliminate a good deal of paper-shuffling, much clerical effort that serves no useful purpose. It would end the rigmarole of taxing Canadians in order to give them as bond interest the money that has just been taken from them by taxation. The amount taken in taxation could be substantially lowered since there would be no need for the government to obtain money with which to pay interest on its Canadian-held bonds. Those people who are alarmed because a large proportion of the government's tax revenue is used to pay the interest on its debt would feel less concern; the government would have to pay interest only on the very small portion of its debt that is held by foreigners. Most important of all, the change would strikingly demonstrate the unique nature of borrowing by a national government from its own citizens, over whom it has unlimited power of taxation.

FOURTEEN

Conclusion

To what purpose is this waste?
MATTHEW 26:8

Probably the bitterest criticism that Karl Marx levelled against the capitalist system was that, to hold wages to the minimum, it maintained an "industrial reserve army of the unemployed." The army, according to Marx, consisted of ragged, hungry wretches standing outside the gate of every factory in the land. Their purpose was to serve as a threat. If ever a worker inside a factory dared to ask for an increase in his miserable pittance of a wage, the owner would point menacingly to the group of wretches standing outside the gate, any one of whom would be overjoyed to trade places with the worker.

Anti-inflation policies of fiscal and monetary restraint validate Marx's criticism. Where they succeed, they do so by causing a degree of unemployment that intimidates unions into moderating their wage demands. Frightened by the large number of people without jobs, workers give priority to security of employment and settle for small pay increases. Restrictive fiscal and monetary policies have the further virtue of being easy to administer, consisting as they do of measures that are simple, impersonal, carried out in bureaucratic offices that are remote from the people they affect: the Bank of Canada simply buys fewer bonds and thereby tightens the national money supply; the government simply allocates less money to some of its programs and thereby reduces its spending.

But while they may be successful against inflation and easy to apply, policies that impose large-scale unemployment involve enormous cost. They cause economic waste in the form of lost output and human trauma in the form of frustration and bitterness, both on an immense scale. And they typically impose the burden of sacrifice primarily upon the community's weakest members – those who have the least market power and are the first victims of overall economic contractions.

The right kind of success in the battle against inflation requires leadership by our national authorities. Businesses cause inflation when they take advantage of their market power to widen their profit margins; trade unions cause inflation when they take advantage of their bargaining power to extract pay raises that exceed productivity growth. These privately achieved gains cause a communal loss in the form of the harm done by inflation to the national economy. That collectively suffered loss exceeds the sum of the private gains, making everybody worse off. What is needed is leadership that persuades individuals to forgo private gains that harm the collectivity and therefore turn out to be against their own best interests. Truly intelligent anti-inflation policy would be made possible by this kind of leadership. Its cornerstone would be a set of arrangements that kept wage and profit increases in Canada in line with the country's productivity growth. They would prevent inflation, without imposing the unemployment caused by fiscal and monetary restraints.

As common sense and experience both affirm, there can be full employment in a country only if there is a sufficient total of spending. The private sector cannot always be relied upon to spend a sufficient amount; at times the necessary aggregate of spending will be reached only if government increases its expenditures or reduces its taxation to promote an increase in private-sector spending, or does both. Tax revenues would then be less than government expenditures.

The federal government could make up the shortfall by simply printing paper currency and creating deposits in the Bank of Canada, as it has the power to do. However, this would almost certainly give rise to inflation. Because the money was so easily obtained, the government would in all probability spend too much. And even if it created only enough money to cover the shortfall, inflation would still occur, because of the nature of our banking system. The currency that the federal authorities can print and the central bank deposits that they can create by the stroke of a pen are the legal "cash" that the chartered banks are required to have as reserves. If the amount of this "cash" is increased, the chartered banks would have larger reserves and would be able to increase their deposits by a multiple of that additional cash. The country's money supply, in the form of deposits in the chartered banks, would increase by more than ten times the amount of money the government had created to cover its revenue shortfall.

It's not necessary for the government to create money. Plenty already exists in the form of savings – money that Canadian individuals and businesses have acquired but don't want to spend now. Savers are prepared to lend their money to someone who will give it back on some agreed-upon future date and, in the meantime, pay them interest. Because of the federal government's absolutely reliable undertaking to pay interest and repay principal, a guarantee that cannot be matched by any other borrower, a good many savers will lend their money to no one else.

Conceivably, the government could simply take money from savers, using its power of appropriation. The governments of some countries have done that. But that is a grossly unfair procedure that penalizes people who have saved their money instead of spending it, and it rewards people who manage to successfully conceal their savings.

If the government puts unemployed people to work by spending money that would otherwise have been saved, it activates productive power that otherwise would have been idle. The country's output becomes larger, with the increase being pure gain; the fact that people don't have to suffer the frustration of unemployment is another and perhaps even larger gain. These gains are not exceeded by monetary costs; the Canadian economy is not so perverse or illogical as to render financially unacceptable undertakings that are physically possible and beneficial to the country. If their financial consequences appear to be negative, it is only because the accounting is incomplete.

We have become caught in a semantic trap. Borrowing by a private individual, a business, a provincial or municipal government, is always and properly a matter of concern since it creates, for the borrowing party, a future obligation of interest payments and principal repayments. The possibility exists that these will prove to be very heavy burdens. It is always better and safer not to have such obligations; if they are unavoidable, it is prudent to keep them to a minimum.

Borrowing by a national government, however, from a bank which it owns and from persons and firms subject to its jurisdiction, has altogether different significance, in light of the power of taxation possessed by the borrowing party over its creditors and its further power to simply create money of the type it owes them. Use of the term "debt" to describe financial obligations of a national government towards its own citizens wrongly implies that it corresponds to the obligations assumed by other types of borrower. Because they make this false analogy, a great many people vehemently oppose borrowing by the federal government that would serve to put unemployed Canadians to productive work, without imposing any burden on the country. In wartime, overriding military necessity brusquely thrust aside the governing myth that a nation courts disaster if it borrows from itself in order to harness fully the country's productive power. With the return of peace, the myth regained its authority.

With effective restraints on inflation firmly in place, it would be safe to apply stimulants that propelled the economy to the full employment level – reductions in interest rates to encourage private-sector borrowing, increases in government spending, reductions in taxation to induce increase in private-sector spending. The effects of increases in government spending and reductions in taxation might be to increase the federal deficit, but, so long as it is financed in Canada, the country will not be burdened.

The people who fiercely oppose the application of employment-generating measures because they might increase the federal deficit are oblivious to the lessons of Canada's wartime and post-war experience. The factual record and contemporary conventional wisdom together make these two declarations:

- Four budget deficits, each equivalent to about $100 billion today, will not create an oppressive burden for the country, provided the money is spent on the production of bombs, shells, and bullets, and on the personnel and vehicles needed to deliver them to an enemy.
- Four budget deficits, if they are in excess of $30 billion, will create enormous economic strains in the present and impose crushing future burdens if the money is spent to build and improve roads, to educate and train young Canadians, to carry on research that will advance our technological capabilities, to encourage increase in private investment, and to generally improve the quality of life in Canada.

Canada's free enterprise system was not devised by a committee of lunatics. It came into being as a rational way of operating an economy, a way that arranges, more effectively than any other system, that the country's productive capacity be used to produce what the general public needs and wants. It does not require that 10 per cent of the country's labour force be unemployed. It does not need war to provide full employment; there can be jobs for all in peace as well as war. What it does require is that the national government use its fiscal power to generate productive jobs for people who would otherwise be idle. And what is needed for this end is emancipation from the paralysing myth that if indeed the government applies the only financial strategy that will prevent the enormous waste and trauma of large-scale unemployment, the country will suffer economic catastrophe.

A clever talker might some day produce ingenious arguments proving that we would be better off if we amputated our right arms. While acknowledging the plausibility of each one of the arguments we would nevertheless refuse to be persuaded; we would feel that this couldn't possibly be right, that there must be some gross omission or misrepresentation in the case put forward. We should feel a similar scepticism towards arguments that demonstrate that it is sound policy to support in idleness one-tenth of Canada's labour force and that the country would be ruined by financial measures that put unemployed people to productive work.

24,95